An Introduction to the Internet for the Older Generation

Jim Gatenby

BERNARD BABANI (publishing) LTD
The Grampians
Shepherds Bush Road
London W6 7NF
England

www.babanibooks.com

D0785380

Please Note

Although every care has been taken with the production of this book to ensure that any projects, designs, modifications and/or programs, etc., contained herewith, operate in a correct and safe manner and also that any components specified are normally available in Great Britain, the Publishers and Author do not accept responsibility in any way for the failure (including fault in design) of any project, design, modification or program to work correctly or to cause damage to any equipment that it may be connected to or used in conjunction with, or in respect of any other damage or injury that may be so caused, nor do the Publishers accept responsibility in any way for the failure to obtain specified components.

Notice is also given that if equipment that is still under warranty is modified in any way or used or connected with home-built equipment then that warranty may be void.

© 2009 BERNARD BABANI (publishing) LTD

First Published – November 2009

British Library Cataloguing in Publication Data:

A catalogue record for this book is available from the British Library

ISBN 978-0-85934-711-2

Cover Design by Gregor Arthur

Printed and bound in Great Britain for Bernard Babani (publishing) Ltd

About This Book

This book is intended to show that older people can benefit greatly from using the Internet; also that the new skills involved are not difficult for anyone to acquire at any age. It's now possible to buy, for under £200, a computer which is perfectly capable of "surfing the net" and opening up a new world of information and entertainment. I genuinely believe that, if used sensibly, the Internet can enhance people's lives and present new opportunities which were previously unimaginable.

The first chapter outlines the main features of the Internet and World Wide Web and discusses some of the many worthwhile applications such as arranging holidays, shopping online, tracing your family history and communicating with friends and family. The second chapter gets down to the nuts and bolts of what you need to get started, the various types of computer, key components and the additional devices needed to make an Internet connection. Chapter Three discusses the choice of Internet Service Providers such as BT and describes how to make an Internet connection using wireless broadband.

The next two chapters discuss the use of a Web browser such as Internet Explorer to find information, view Web pages and revisit Web sites at a later date. Alternative browsers such as Mozilla Firefox are also discussed, together with the Microsoft "ballot screen" which presents users with a choice of browsers to install.

Electronic mail enables people all over the world to communicate and exchange information, including the sending of photographs. This is described in detail together with the creation of your own Web presence in the form of a "blog" (or "Web log") or a simple personal Web site. The final chapter describes some simple steps to keep your computer up-to-date and protected from viruses and criminal activities such as "phishing".

This book is suitable for users of all versions of Microsoft Windows, including Microsoft XP, Vista and Windows 7.

About the Author

Jim Gatenby trained as a Chartered Mechanical Engineer and initially worked at Rolls-Royce Ltd using computers in the analysis of jet engine performance. He obtained a Master of Philosophy degree in Mathematical Education by research at Loughborough University of Technology and taught mathematics and computing in school for many years before becoming a full-time author. The author has written many books in the fields of educational computing and Microsoft Windows, including many of the titles in the highly successful Older Generation series from Bernard Babani (publishing) Ltd.

The author has considerable experience of teaching students of all ages and abilities, in school and in adult education. For several years he successfully taught the well-established CLAIT course and also GCSE Computing and Information Technology.

Trademarks

Microsoft, Windows, Windows XP, Windows Vista, Windows 7, Windows Mail, Microsoft Word and Excel are either trademarks or registered trademarks of Microsoft Corporation. Kaspersky internet Security is a trademark of Kaspersky Lab. Mozilla, Firefox and Thunderbird are trademarks of the Mozilla Foundation. Norton AntiVirus and Norton 360 are trademarks of Symantec Corporation. F-Secure Internet Security is a trademark or registered trademark of F-Secure Corporation. AVG Anti-Virus is a trademark or registered trademark of AVG Technologies. BT is a registered trademark of British Telecommunications plc. WebPlus is a trademark of Serif (Europe) Ltd.

All other brand and product names used in this book are recognized as trademarks or registered trademarks, of their respective companies.

This book is by the same author as the best-selling and highly acclaimed "Computing for the Older Generation" (BP601).

Contents

3

4

5

More Surfing and Searching

Conventions Used in this Book

Words which appear on the screen in menus, etc., are shown in the text in bold, for example, **Print Preview**.

Technical terms for devices which may be unfamiliar to the reader are introduced in italics, for example, *wireless router*. Many of these terms appear in the glossary on page 113.

If a word appears on the screen using the American spelling, such as **Favorites**, for example, this spelling is also used in the text of the book.

Mouse Operation

Throughout this book, the following terms are used to describe the operation of the mouse:

Click

A single press of the left-hand mouse button.

Double-click

Two presses of the left-hand mouse button, in rapid succession.

Right-click

A single press of the right-hand mouse button. This can be used to display *context-sensitive* menus, i.e. relevant to the objects on the screen at the current cursor position.

Drag and Drop

Keep the left-hand or right-hand button held down and move the mouse, before releasing the button to transfer a screen object to a new position.

Further Reading

If you enjoy reading this book and find it helpful, you may be interested in the companion book by the same author, **Getting Started in Computing for the Older Generation (BP704)** from Bernard Babani (publishing) Ltd and available from all good bookshops.

Introduction

Age Doesn't Matter

The media often give the impression that older people can't really cope with computers and that new technology is the exclusive preserve of the young. This false impression causes many older people to mistakenly think they've missed the boat. However, having taught students of all ages from eleven to eighty, I know that age is no barrier to making good use of computers in general and the *Internet* in particular. Older people usually have more time to learn new computing skills and the wisdom and experience to apply these skills to worthwhile activities. For example, since retiring from teaching I have written nearly 30 books, including the best-selling and highly-acclaimed "Computing for the Older Generation".

You're Never Too Old

A friend of mine, Arthur, is now 77 years old and is the computer "guru" for many of the people in his locality. He also manages all of the computers at a nearby religious centre. Arthur's regular computing activities include:

- Building new machines to customers' requirements.
- Repairing and upgrading computers.
- Setting up connections to the Internet.
- Downloading *software*, music and video from the Internet.

Although everyone doesn't need Arthur's level of technical expertise, the following pages are intended to show how you can get started with the Internet and use it for a wide range of enjoyable and beneficial activities, no matter how old you are.

It's Never Been Easier

Nowadays with hand-held *mice* and onscreen *menus* and *icons*, many tasks just require you to "point and click", as shown on the right. Simply move the mouse so that the arrow-shaped cursor is over the required menu  option and click the left button on the mouse. Clicking the right mouse button usually brings up a *context sensitive* menu, i.e. relevant to the current cursor position.

While computers have become much easier to use, they have also become more affordable; you can now buy a small *netbook computer* for around £200, which is quite suitable for most Internet tasks, as discussed later in this book.

Special Needs

If you have any physical problems such as poor eyesight or impaired dexterity, you can tailor the computer to your needs using the *Ease of Access Center* in the Windows *Control Panel*. This is discussed in more detail in our companion book, Getting Started in Computing for the Older Generation from Bernard Babani (publishing) Ltd, reference BP 704.

Ease of Access Center

Make your computer easier to use

Quick access to common tools
You can use the tools in this section to help you get started.

Windows can read and scan this list automatically. Press the SPACEBAR to select the highlighted tool.

☑ Always read this section aloud   ☐ Always scan this section

Start Magnifier   Start Narrator

Start On-Screen Keyboard   Set up High Contrast

What is the Internet?

The Internet is a network of millions of computers all over the world. They are connected by various methods in order to communicate information, along what is sometimes called *The Information Superhighway*. Many computers are connected to the Internet by telephone lines while others use wireless networks, satellite communication or cable television networks. People on the move can use a **laptop** computer to connect to the Internet via an **access point** in a hotel or airport, for example, while others may use a mobile phone network. Some mobile phones can themselves be used to connect to the Internet.

Internet Servers

A **server** is a computer on a network (such as the Internet) which stores information for other people to view on their own computer. For example, large stores display information on their servers allowing customers to view products and make purchases **online**, i.e. while connected to the Internet.

Internet Service Providers

Many servers are located at specialist Internet companies known as **Internet Service Providers**, usually abbreviated to **ISP**. These are companies, such as BT, AOL and Tiscali, for example, who manage users' connections to the Internet. ISPs provide a **user name** and **password** to allow you to log on to the Internet and also use facilities for sending **e-mails**; these are electronic messages sent to other people with a computer on the Internet. Some Internet Service Providers also include their own *content* on their servers, such as pages of news and information.

Information on the Internet

The Internet is like an encyclopaedia of unimaginable size and scope. Servers around the world contain information on every conceivable subject; unlike the encyclopaedia it can be kept up-to-date in a matter of minutes. This information is generally available to anyone with a computer and an Internet connection.

The World Wide Web, Web Pages and Sites

Information on the Internet usually takes the form of pages, similar to pages in a book and the entire global collection of pages is known as the **World Wide Web** or **WWW**; a **Web site** is a set of **Web pages** belonging to a company or individual. Web pages can consist of various types of information, such as:

- Plain text presenting paragraphs of facts.
- Pictures, diagrams, charts and photographic images.
- **Links** which you click with a mouse to move to other Web pages or to play sound, music or watch TV or video.

No-one is in overall control of the Internet; some Web sites require you to register and set up a user name and password while others charge a fee for viewing certain Web pages.

Downloading

It's often useful to be able to copy a report, some music or a video, for example, from an Internet server and save a duplicate copy on your own computer. This is known as **downloading**.

Uploading

Uploading involves sending information from your computer and saving it on another machine on the Internet. For example, some Internet servers allow you to save your photographs on the Web so that anyone can view them from anywhere in the world. Uploading is generally a slower process than downloading.

E-mail

This is a major use of the Internet and is the sending and receiving of messages as an alternative to the traditional letter post; e-mail is very quick and easy to use. Pictures, photographs and reports can be attached to an e-mail and sent electronically. As discussed later, there are many other Web sites that allow people to communicate, express their views and exchange ideas.

Searching for Information

One of the most powerful facilities of the Internet is the ability to find the latest information on virtually any subject by simply typing in one or more *keywords*. Most computers have a program called a *Web browser*, which helps you to search the Internet and move about its many Web pages. Internet Explorer is probably the most popular browser and includes a Search Bar into which you type your keywords. Shown below is a search to find information about the **peregrine falcon**, for example.

When you click the magnifying glass icon or press the **Enter** key a list of Web sites is displayed, each containing information about the **peregrine falcon**. When you click any of the links in the list (usually shown underlined) the corresponding Web site is opened up. As shown above, you can also focus your search on particular categories such as **News**, **Images** and **Maps**, etc.

Google is a very popular program dedicated to searching the Internet and is known as a *search engine*. It can be installed on your computer after opening the Web page **www.google.co.uk**.

Searching with Google is discussed in detail later in this book.

Some Popular Internet Activities

The remainder of this chapter gives a taste of some of the most popular applications of the Internet. Some of these are discussed in more detail in later chapters.

Booking a Holiday

Some of the main features of holiday Web sites are:

- You can view the rooms, prices and hotel facilities.
- Sample restaurant menus can be perused.
- You can see videos and notes on the surrounding area.
- Vacancies can be checked immediately.
- Bookings can be made online and quickly confirmed.

 HOTEL CIPRIANI ▶VENICE   LOCATION   THE HOTEL   PALAZZI   DINING

Events Calendar | History | Weather & Tides

A GUIDE TO VENICE

Leave the tourist trail behind and discover the city with the guidance of our Concierge to the unexpected landmarks, shops and restaurants

Dining in Venice
Dining is an essential part of any visit to Venice, plan a long casual lunch, or that romantic dinner for two.
more »

 The Sights of Venice
Use our interactive map to g off the beaten track and enj some exceptional sights of Venice.
more »

The Weekly Shopping Online

Online shopping allows you to browse catalogues and purchase books, groceries, music, etc., from the comfort of your own home. Major supermarkets such as Tesco and Sainsburys have built up significant online shopping enterprises, saving you the time and effort of the weekly shopping trip.

After completing your initial order online (in only a few minutes), the system "remembers" your shopping list and this can be used as the basis for your future weekly shopping. In subsequent weeks you only have to select any new items and confirm or omit the items on your basic core list. When your order is complete you select a convenient delivery time; the most popular delivery "slots" are slightly more expensive.

Online shopping can literally reduce an entire week's shopping to just a few minutes at the computer.

Tracing Your Family History

Much of the census information for the United Kingdom has been placed on the Internet for anyone to see. Original census transcripts are available to be viewed and printed for a small fee and it's also possible to obtain copies of original birth, marriage and death certificates.

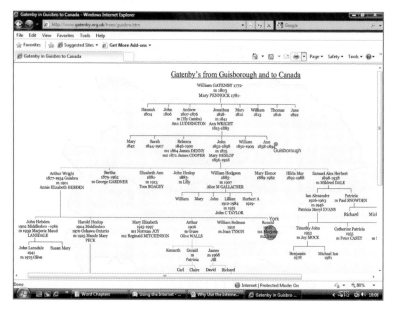

There are many Web sites offering help with genealogy; some of these allow you to post up notices asking for information from relatives anywhere in the world. There are also Web sites listing parish records and enabling you to construct your own family tree. Shown above is part of my own family tree which contains information about ancestors I would never otherwise have known about. Without the Internet such work would be extremely difficult and time-consuming, but the Internet brings masses of information within your grasp without even leaving home.

Buying and Selling on eBay

If you are thinking of downsizing or simply want to get rid of some "clutter", **eBay** allows you to offer your items to a nationwide or even worldwide audience of over 200 million potential customers. The range of goods offered for sale on eBay is enormous, from jewellery, antiques, porcelain and collectable items through to motor vehicles and even aircraft. As shown below, each item is listed with a photograph and a brief description.

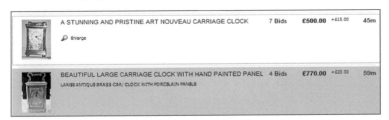

A time limit for the sale, usually several days, is set by the seller and eBay displays a running total of the number of bids, the highest bid received so far and the amount of time left for bidding. The cost of posting the item in the United Kingdom is also shown on the screen. At the end of the time allowed for bidding, the item is sold to the highest bidder who must then pay for the item before the seller arranges delivery by normal post. Obviously in the case of very large items such as cars or furniture, buyer and seller must liaise to agree viewing and make arrangements for collection.

PayPal is a security system used by eBay to protect the purchaser's payment against the goods not being delivered and also ensures that the seller receives their payment instantly. A feature called **Meet the seller** allows you to check their record, including the number of transactions made and a rating based on the amount of positive feedback from other users.

Electronic Greeting Cards

Instead of sending an e-mail message consisting of just plain text, a more interesting option is to send an *e-card;* this is rather like a traditional greeting card displayed on a screen but with sound and music and animations including birds and animals. The Jacquie Lawson range of cards (**www.jacquielawson.com**) offers a wide choice of e-cards covering every type of greeting or message you are likely to send throughout the entire year. The e-card graphics and animations are both amusing and designed to a very high standard, as shown in the extract below.

There is a small annual membership fee and this enables you to send as many cards as you wish throughout the year. Once you've selected a card it can be previewed and then the e-mail addresses of your intended recipients are entered. After adding a few words for your own personal message, the e-card can be finally previewed and the **Send Card** button clicked to send the card electronically on its way.

Interactive Web Sites and Social Networking

In recent years a number of Web sites have been set up to allow anyone to post their own material (such as text, photos and videos) on the Internet, for anyone to see and comment on. Most of these Web sites are completely free although you may have to register and accept the terms and conditions laid down by the Web site providers. You usually have to set up a user name and password. The providers of the Web site are obliged to remove offensive material and ban irresponsible users; individual users can also report anyone they think is abusing the Web site, for example by posting offensive comments or obscene images.

Facebook and MySpace are very popular Web sites which enable people to acquire new friends and communicate with them online. A personal profile including photos and videos may be uploaded to the Web site. Facebook and MySpace are examples of *social networking* Web sites.

Twitter allows you to keep friends and family up-to-date with what you are currently doing; you do this by posting *tweets* or short text messages of up to 140 characters in length.

Friends Reunited helps you to make contact with old friends and classmates and let them know what you have done with your life since leaving school.

Flickr is a Web site for posting your photographs and videos on the Internet; there are powerful photo-editing tools and facilities to organize your photographs into categories so they can be shared with other like-minded people.

YouTube is a Web site which allows you to upload videos and share them with other people; these can be amateur clips or videos recorded from TV programs and concerts. Amusing or embarrassing incidents can be captured on video and very quickly viewed by millions around the world.

The Diversity of the Internet

The following are some of the ways my own family uses the Internet; without the Internet, many of the tasks would take much longer and some would be impossible.

- Sending e-mails to friends and family.
- Booking holidays after checking vacancies and viewing the accommodation and surrounding area online.
- Tracking flight arrivals and departures at various airports.
- Checking-in online, avoiding airport queuing.
- Ordering the weekly shopping in a few minutes online.
- Using an online census to find details of forebears.
- Ordering books online, delivered the next day.
- Validating the ownership history of a second-hand car.
- Valuing a car and renewing road tax online.
- Selling surplus household items on eBay.
- Downloading software and music.
- Finding information about plants and shrubs.
- Finding best interest rates on Internet bank accounts.
- Checking current account bank statements, setting up standing orders and transferring funds online.
- Searching for houses and flats in other parts of Britain.
- Ordering repeat prescriptions from local Medical Centre.
- Filing self-assessment income tax online.
- Obtaining state pensions information and forecast online.
- Identifying birds by viewing RSPB images and videos.
- Solving obscure crossword clues.
- Sending electronic animated greeting cards or e-cards.

Everything You Need

Introduction

This chapter describes the equipment and other facilities needed to start using the Internet in your own home or on the move. The essential requirements are:

- A computer of fairly recent manufacture.

- Access to an Internet source such as a BT landline, TV cable network or a mobile phone network.

- A *modem* or device for connecting the computer to the Internet; alternatively several computers can connect using a *router*, a sharing device with a built-in modem.

- A *Web browser* i.e. software for searching for information, displaying Web pages and moving between the pages. Most computers already have the Internet Explorer browser installed and others are freely available.

- An account with an Internet Service Provider (ISP), who manages your Internet connection and provides e-mail facilities and perhaps news and information content.

- Additional software may be needed to play music, video and radio and TV programs. This software, known as *plug-ins*, can be downloaded free from the Internet.

The next few pages discuss the setting up of an Internet computer in the home. It should be pointed out that most computers made in the last few years will be suitable for use on the Internet. It's also true that no great technical skills or knowledge are required — you probably won't even need to use a screwdriver.

Microsoft Windows

You have probably heard the terms ***Windows XP***, ***Windows Vista*** and ***Windows 7***; Microsoft Windows is a suite of ***programs*** known as an ***operating system***. It is the software which controls every aspect of the running of a computer, such as saving and printing your work and displaying information on the screen. The computer is operated by clicking ***icons*** (or small pictures) and ***menu options*** displayed in various rectangular boxes or ***windows***. This is called a Graphical User Interface.

The Windows PC (or Personal Computer) dominates home and business computing throughout the world; currently either Windows XP, Windows Vista or the latest version, Windows 7, are installed on the majority of personal computers. Microsoft Windows has a Web browser, ***Internet Explorer*** (currently at version 8), which is used to search for and display Web pages; other browsers, such as Mozilla Firefox, can be installed and used with Windows, as discussed later. To find which version of Windows is installed on your computer, click the **Start** button, shown on the right, then **Computer** (click **My Computer** in Windows XP) and then **System properties**. In Windows XP select **View system information**.

View basic information about your computer

Windows edition

Windows 7 Ultimate

Copyright © 2009 Microsoft Corporation. All rights reserved.

This book covers Windows XP, Vista and Windows 7; where there are differences these are explained in the text.

The Internet Computer

The speed with which you can find Web pages and move between them is important; if it's too slow you may become bored and lose interest. One critical factor affecting the speed of the Internet is the type of connection, which can be either an early **dial-up** system or a much faster and more modern **broadband** connection. These are discussed in detail shortly, but unless you are on a very tight budget, a broadband connection will enable you to get the best out of the Internet.

If buying a new computer, the choice nowadays is between a full size desktop machine and a laptop. In recent years laptop computers have improved a great deal so that they are now comparable with desktop machines in terms of performance.

The Desktop Computer

If you are going to do other work on your computer such as word processing or accounts, for example, perhaps in a home office, then a desktop machine is probably the best choice. The desktop computer has the advantage of a full size keyboard, mouse and monitor, as shown below.

The Laptop Computer

For using the Internet on the move in hotels and airports, etc., the laptop computer is the only choice. These public places now have Internet *access points*, enabling you to connect to the Internet using the wireless technology built into modern laptops.

The Netbook Computer

The *netbook* is a very small laptop computer, typically 10 inches or less across the screen (measured diagonally), compared with 15 inches for a normal laptop. Despite its very small size, the typical netbook performs as well as many much larger desktop machines. (If the small screen is a problem you can increase the text size using the **Zoom** or **Text Size** options on the **View** menu in Internet Explorer). If necessary the netbook can be connected to a full size keyboard, mouse and monitor. A typical netbook is shown below to the right of a normal-sized laptop computer.

Laptop and netbook computers are usually "Internet ready"; they can easily be connected to the Internet via a *wireless router* or Internet *access point*. Simply switch on the computer's *WiFi* and enter a security key or password (as discussed shortly).

Computer Performance

Although you don't need an expensive super computer to make good use of the Internet, a sluggish machine will spoil your surfing experience.

Three of the most critical components affecting the performance of a computer are the **processor**, the **memory** (also known as **RAM**) and the **hard disc drive**.

The Processor

Often described as the brains of a computer, the processor can also be likened to the engine room of a ship which powers everything else. The processor carries out millions of instructions when executing a program; the speed of a processor is measured in **gigahertz (GHz)** or thousands of millions of cycles per second. While many new machines have processor speeds of around 3 GHz, any machine with a processor speed of 1 GHz or above should be fine for Internet use. An AMD Athlon processor chip is shown on the right.

The Memory or RAM

The memory stores the instructions and data which are being used by the current program, which might be an Internet Web browser or search engine, for example. If a computer has insufficient memory for a particular task, the computer will run very slowly. Memory or RAM is measured in **megabytes (MB)** or **gigabytes (GB)** which stand for millions and thousands of millions of characters respectively. A character is a letter of the alphabet or digit 0-9, etc. New machines are currently being delivered with 3 or 4GB of RAM but this is not essential for general Internet use. Machines running the Windows Vista operating system need at least 1GB of RAM but preferably 2GB. For the earlier Windows XP operating system 512MB should be quite adequate. 1GB of RAM is recommended for Windows 7 (for the 32-bit version) and I have found this quite adequate.

Increasing the memory is a simple and inexpensive job which can yield very pleasing improvements in performance. It's just a case of removing the cover of the computer and either fitting an extra memory module (shown on the right) or replacing a module with one of a higher capacity.

The Hard Disc Drive

This is a set of magnetic discs inside the computer, revolving at very high speed. The hard disc is the permanent store for all of your programs and data files including copies of Web

pages which you've recently visited. The hard disc is also used as temporary storage when a computer has insufficient memory (RAM) for the current task. A computer will run badly if the hard disc is nearly full. New computers may have a hard disc capacity of 250 or even 500GB but most users can manage with less.

Shown below are the specifications of four inexpensive home computers. These machines are not particularly powerful or state of the art, but they are all used to surf the Internet quite happily without any frustrating delays waiting for pages to load.

Windows Version	Processor Speed (GHz)	Memory (RAM)	Hard Disc Capacity (GB)
XP (Netbook)	1.6	448MB	68.5
XP (Laptop)	1.4	512MB	40
Vista (Desktop)	2.6	2GB	149
Windows 7(Desktop)	1.6	1GB	76.6

Examining the Specification of a Computer

To check the specification of a computer, click the **Start** button shown on the right and then click **Computer** in

Windows Vista or Windows 7. (In Windows XP click **Start** and **My Computer**). The size of the hard disc and the free space are revealed, as shown on the right.

70% free (1)

Local Disk (C:)

104 GB free of 149 GB

Now click **System properties** in Vista or Windows 7 (in Windows XP click **View System Information**) to check the amount of **Memory (RAM)** and the speed (GHz) of the **Processor**.

System	
Rating:	**3.1** Windows Experience Index
Processor:	AMD Athlon(tm) Processor LE-1640 2.60 GHz
Memory (RAM):	2.00 GB
System type:	32-bit Operating System

It Needn't Cost the Earth

You don't need to spend a fortune on an Internet computer; the desktop machine running Windows Vista shown in the table on the previous page cost under £300 new, including a slimline TFT monitor. Netbook computers can be bought for around £200, as discussed shortly and you won't need to spend much else, apart from a monthly subscription to an Internet Service Provider.

Buying Second Hand

You could probably pick up an adequate second hand machine for £100 or less. These may be advertised in your local paper or on eBay, for example. Second hand electrical goods in particular need to be carefully checked before buying and it may be advisable to take along a knowledgeable friend. However, having had numerous computers over many years I have found them to be incredibly reliable with no expensive repairs needed.

Adding a Printer

Once you start using the Internet, you'll probably find you need a printer to make hard copies of Web pages to read away from the computer. Also many Web sites provide copies of documents such as notes and booklets on taxation or health matters or user manuals for equipment and software; these are posted on the Internet as **Portable Document Format (PDF)** files which can be downloaded to your computer and printed out on paper. The advantage of PDF files is that they can be read on any computer and you don't need special software such as Microsoft Word to read them. All you need is a program called Adobe Reader, which can be downloaded free of charge from the Internet and installed on your computer. Downloading and installing software such as Adobe Reader is a simple task, as discussed later.

Shown below is an example of a multi-function inkjet printer. These produce good quality output for both text and images, including photographs. The multi-function title means the printer also doubles up as an easy-to-use colour photocopier for documents and photographs; you can also **scan** documents and save the scanned image as a file on your hard disc or insert it in a program such as a word processor.

Although a scanned image of a text document is like a photograph and can't normally be edited, some scanners have an OCR facility which converts the image into text which can then be edited in a text editing program. Scanned images can also be sent electronically as e-mail **attachments**. This would be useful if you had some old photographic prints and wanted  to e-mail copies to friends or relatives in Australia, for example.

Internet Connections — Dial-up vs. Broadband

There are two main systems for delivering the Internet to your computer, known as *dial-up* and **broadband**. Dial-up is the original method of making a connection and was widely used until a few years ago. Although some people still use a dial-up connection, it has been overtaken by broadband, for the following reasons:

- Broadband is many times faster than dial-up, giving better searching and display of Web pages and enabling large photographs, music and video files, etc., to be uploaded and downloaded more quickly.

- You can use a broadband connection and an ordinary telephone handset simultaneously, using the same telephone socket. With dial-up it's one or the other. This can be very inconvenient if you only have one BT line.

- The broadband connection is always on throughout the day, whereas with dial-up your computer needs to dial the Internet server's telephone number for every session.

Some people may choose to continue with a dial-up Internet service rather than graduate to broadband because:

- The subscription to an Internet Service Provider for a dial-up service is usually much cheaper than for broadband.

- The speed of the dial-up service may be adequate for their particular Internet activities, especially if they don't want to download or upload very large multi-media files.

- In a few areas of Britain a broadband service may not be available because the local telephone exchange has not been modified to deliver broadband.

The Dial-up Modem

A **dial-up modem** is a device that converts the *digital* information from a computer into the *analogue* format used by the telephone lines. An external dial-up modem is a small box which plugs into a standard BT telephone socket. Another cable from the modem connects to one of the **USB**  ports on the computer, as shown on the right. Some dial-up modems connect to the *COM* or *serial ports*, i.e. sockets, on the computer, as shown on the right. An internal dial-up modem takes the form of a small *expansion card*, a plug-in circuit board inside the computer. Many computers already have an internal dial-up modem built in; if not, a dial-up modem can be bought for a few pounds.

The Broadband Modem

Broadband requires a special **ADSL modem**; this stands for **Asymmetric Digital Subscriber Line**. *Asymmetric* refers to the fact that it's much faster to receive information into your computer than to send it up to the Internet. Like the dial-up modem, the ADSL modem can still use the ordinary copper telephone cables but data is transferred at much higher speeds. In addition telephone exchanges need to be modified to offer a broadband service. This has been the stumbling block preventing some areas receiving broadband.

One cable from the ADSL modem connects to one of the **USB ports** on the computer as shown above; another cable connects the ADSL modem to a telephone socket via a **splitter** or **microfilter** shown on the right. The splitter enables you to use the Internet at the same time as making a telephone call; this may be useful if you are expecting a phone call while using the Internet or to seek computing help using a telephone helpline.

The Wireless Router

Many homes now have more than one computer, especially with the increased sales of laptop and netbook computers. The **wireless router** is a device which enables one broadband-activated telephone line to be *shared* wirelessly between several computers; the router may contain a built-in ADSL modem or the modem may be a separate device.

Some networks use special **Ethernet cables** to connect computers and wireless routers generally have some sockets for Ethernet cables, so it's possible to have a mixed wireless and cabled network. Many businesses still use cable networks as they are very fast; however, for the home user, wireless networks are a better solution as they avoid the need to drill holes in walls and have wires trailing around the home. The wireless router needs to be situated near to a telephone socket in your home. Once the network is up and running the computers can be used anywhere in the house, flat or garden; the wireless signals, i.e. radio waves, can penetrate several walls and floors.

Wireless routers may have a built-in **firewall** to prevent hackers getting access to your computer. The firewall is a program stored in the permanent memory of the router. This type of program is known as **firmware**; although regarded as semi-permanent, it is possible to update a firmware program with a later version.

Wireless routers are often provided free when you sign up with an Internet Service Provider; even if you only have one laptop or netbook computer, the wireless router is an excellent way to get online.

The BT Home Hub shown on the next page is a popular wireless router and includes a built-in ADSL modem. Diagnostic lights on the front of the Hub indicate when broadband and wireless are working correctly and when upgrading is taking place. There is also a button to restart the router; this sometimes provides the solution to a connection problem.

Ports on a Router

Shown on the right is the rear of a wireless router, in this case the BT Home Hub. Above the row of ports or sockets is a label giving various security details for the router, intended to prevent other people using the connection to the Internet which you are paying for. These are the **Network name** or **SSID** (Service Set Identifier) and the **Wireless key**. Whenever someone tries to connect to your network for the  first time, they need to enter the wireless key. Otherwise anyone nearby such as a neighbour or impecunious student with a laptop in the street outside could use your Internet connection.

The white left-hand socket in the group of sockets above is used for the cable which connects the router to the broadband telephone socket, via a filter, as mentioned previously. The green socket is for connecting a telephone handset. The four yellow Ethernet sockets have several uses, such as the initial setting up of the router using an Ethernet cable connected to a computer. The Ethernet sockets can also be used to create a *wired network,* using Ethernet cables and adaptors instead of wireless technology. A further use of one of the Ethernet sockets is for a cable to connect the BT Vision digital box, as discussed on page 31. On the right of the router above is the socket for the power cable; finally there is a USB socket to connect a cable to a USB port on a computer (as an alternative to an Ethernet cable.) This might be used in the initial setting up process before your wireless connection is working.

Wireless Network Adaptors

Each computer on the wireless network must have some form of *wireless network adaptor* fitted. This enables the network computer to send and receive information from the router. Laptop and netbook computers normally have this technology built-in as standard enabling them to get straight onto the Internet. A desktop machine may need a wireless network adaptor which can be bought for a few pounds and fitted quite easily.

The Wireless Dongle

The adaptor can be in the form of a *dongle* as shown below. This plugs into a USB port on the front or back of the computer, as shown on page 22.

The wireless dongle above is shown plugged into a desktop stand with a USB extension cable; although the dongle may be plugged directly into a USB port on the computer, the extension cable allows you to move the dongle around to optimize the strength of the wireless signal.

The Wireless Adaptor Card

Alternatively the wireless network adaptor may be an *expansion card* as shown below. This fits inside the computer case. There is also a small aerial which can be moved around to optimize the signal strength. Network adaptors should be compatible with a **Wi-Fi** standard known as **802.11b**, **g**, or **n**.

Fitting a wireless network adaptor card is not difficult; it's simply a case of taking the cover off the computer and carefully pushing the card into one of the spare *PCI slots* on the computer's *motherboard*, the large circuit board to which everything else connects.

A network adaptor dongle or card may be included in a wireless router package and they can be purchased for under £10 from computer shops and by mail order. The package should also include installation instructions and a CD containing the *driver software* needed to make the device work with your computer.

Internet Service Providers

Introduction

An **Internet Service Provider (ISP)** is a company which manages connections to the Internet for individual users. This is done using powerful computers known as **Web servers**. Apart from enabling you to search the World Wide Web and display Web pages, the ISP usually also provides your e-mail facilities. Some Internet Service Providers also have their own Web pages displaying content such as news, sport and the weather. The choice of Internet Service Providers is huge, although there are a few household names which dominate the market such as BT, O_2, Virgin Media, TalkTalk, AOL and the Post Office. Most broadband is delivered through the BT telephone network, alternatives being fibre optic television cables (Virgin Media), satellite, local wireless networks and the mobile telephone network. Not all services are available in every area.

If you already have access to the Internet, there are some useful Web sites which compare ISPs and also tell you which types of broadband are available in your area. If you don't yet have Internet access, your local library may provide Internet computers enabling you to log on and do your own research.

Broadband | checker

Broadband Summary

Broadband services for the YZ63 7PQ area on 23rd June 2009

ADSL ✔ ADSL Broadband using a standard BT line is available

Cable ✘ Cable Broadband is not available from the service providers we checked

Satellite ✔ Satellite TV + Broadband is available

Mobile 3G ✔ Mobile Broadband for your PC using wireless 3G

Broadband services may be subject to additional line tests and available network capacity in your area.

Shown on the previous page is an extract from the Broadband checker Web site at **www.broadbandchecker.co.uk**. After entering your post code, the Web page displays the Internet services available in your area. The extract shows that my area is served by ADSL broadband using a BT line from the local telephone exchange, which has been broadband "enabled". This may not always be the case in some remote areas. The Broadband checker extract also shows that cable broadband is not available in the area but satellite and mobile broadband are.

The Broadband checker also lists a number of Internet Service Providers available in the area. There are several other broadband comparison Web sites on the Internet such as Top 10 Broadband at **www.top10-broadband.co.uk**, shown in the extract below. After entering your post code this shows broadband services available in your area.

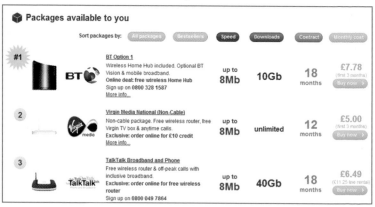

If you've not yet got access to an Internet computer, perhaps you could enlist an Internet "savvy" friend or relative who can help you look at the various comparison Web sites. You could also ask them about their own choice of ISP. Our own Internet Service Provider for the last few years has been BT Broadband and we have seen no reason to change; the service has always been very reliable and there is good telephone support.

Choosing an Internet Service Provider

You can see from the previous table the criteria on which Internet Service Providers are compared; some suppliers offer various packages such as light, heavy or unlimited Internet usage. The following list suggests some criteria to compare Internet Service Providers and perhaps discuss with more experienced friends.

Criteria for Choosing an Internet Service Provider

- Availability of a broadband service in your area.
- The monthly subscription.
- The speed for downloading information.
- The amount of downloading "traffic" allowed per month.
- The minimum length of your contract with the ISP.
- The reliability of the service — freedom from "down-time".
- Quality and availability of telephone and e-mail support.
- Cost or ease of setting up the Internet connection initially.
- Any special signing on offers such as a free wireless router, mobile modem "dongle" or free laptop computer.
- Provision of free Internet security and anti-virus software.
- Any penalties or difficulties if changing to another ISP.

Download Speed

This is important because it is the speed at which Web pages open on the screen and large files such as music and video can be transferred to your computer from the Internet.

Download speeds are measured in *Megabits* per second (Mbps) or millions of *bits* per second. A character or letter of the alphabet occupies about 10 bits.

Many Internet Service Providers are currently offering speeds of up to 8 or 10Mbps, with others offering 2Mbps, 20Mbps and Virgin Media offering 50Mbps over *fibre optic* cables.

Monthly Charges for Broadband

Although the first 3 months may be at a reduced rate, typically £5-£8 per month, after that you can expect to pay more like £15-£20 for a limited amount of usage with nearer £25-£30 for unlimited downloads. If you exceed your monthly download allowance of, say, 10GB of information downloaded, you are charged for the extra usage.

Contract

You are normally required to enter into an agreement to pay the subscription for either 12 or 18 months. There may be a cooling off period allowing you to cancel the agreement and obtain a refund but you may be expected to return any free equipment provided as part of the initial offer. Your chosen ISP package should allow you to set up one or more e-mail accounts and may also provide server space for you to create your own Web site.

Dial-Up Internet Services

Although broadband now dominates the advertisements in newspapers and magazines, dial-up users are still catered for. A dial-up service may be adequate if you are only a light Internet user with just a small amount of Web browsing each week and perhaps some e-mailing. All you need is a dial-up modem which plugs into a port on your computer and this connects to the Internet via an ordinary, unmodified phone line. Some dial-up services are free, i.e. there is no monthly subscription, although you will have to pay your telephone company for the time the line is used. This should be charged at the rate for local telephone calls. Tiscali, now part of TalkTalk, at the time of writing offered a pay-as-you-go dial-up service charged at 1p for each minute surfing the net while another package allowed up to 150 hours a month for a fixed monthly fee of £14.99.

It should be remembered that a dial-up connection will not allow you to download large image or video files unless you are prepared to wait a very long time — hours rather than minutes.

Other ISP Services

As well as providing and managing your Internet connection and e-mail services, some Internet Service Providers offer other related services, such as:

Phones

Some broadband packages, such as BT, Sky and Tiscali, include cheap or unlimited evening and weekend phone calls.

Digital Television

Both Sky and BT offer a digital television service. We have been using BT Vision for about two years and have found it to be a giant leap forward compared with earlier systems, in terms of ease of use, speed, reliability and powerful features. The BT Vision television service offered with BT Broadband includes a free digital television recorder box. The box has a built-in 160GB hard disc. The TV box and the BT Home Hub are connected either by an Ethernet cable or by wireless adaptors. If necessary you can pay to have BT Vision installed by a BT engineer, but it's not difficult to do the job yourself. Among the many features of BT Vision are:

- Pausing and restarting of live television.
- Over 70 FreeView TV and radio channels available.
- The ability to record up to 80 hours of TV programs.
- *Scheduled* recording of TV programs including *series*.
- Record two programs simultaneously including the one you are currently watching.
- Easy replaying and eventual deletion of recordings.
- Films, TV programs and sport, etc., available *on demand* for downloading at any time, for an extra charge.
- Constantly updated *TV Guide* giving program schedules for two weeks ahead.

Making an Internet Connection

After reviewing the various broadband options and packages available in your area you need to sign up for an account with an Internet Service Provider. Apart from BT themselves, many other ISPs use the BT telephone lines to deliver their service; regardless of which ISP you are using, before you can connect to the Internet your broadband ADSL line must be *activated* in your local telephone exchange by a BT engineer. This may take about a week and there may be an activation charge.

Setting Up a Wireless Router

This is a very popular method of connecting to the Internet via an ADSL i.e. "broadband-enabled" telephone line. It allows one or more computers to get access to the Internet from anywhere in your home or garden, without the need to drill holes in walls and trail untidy cables around the rooms.

As well as a free wireless router, ISPs may also provide one or more *microfilters* or *splitters* to allow the Internet to be used at the same time as an ordinary telephone. The microfilter has two sockets, one to accept a cable from the router and one for a cable from the telephone handset. A short cable from the microfilter plugs into the telephone socket on the wall. BT recommend fitting a microfilter to every telephone socket in your home. The filter prevents interference from other electrical devices which may be plugged into telephone sockets.

As mentioned in Chapter 2, each computer on a wireless network needs to be fitted with a wireless network adaptor; modern laptops and netbooks have this wireless capability built in as standard, although it may need to be switched on. The wireless switch may be on the front or side of a laptop. Some desktop machines may need a wireless network adaptor to be fitted, at a cost of a few pounds.

Your Internet Service Provider should send you clear instructions for connecting the router and its various cables. Once connected the power to the router is switched on and all being well the diagnostic lights on the router should indicate everything is operating correctly. The next step is to place a computer near to the router, start it up and insert the CD provided by your ISP. Now follow the instructions on the screen.

If, perhaps to understand your system better, you prefer to use a manual approach to setting up a wireless broadband router, you can use the **Connect to a network** feature in Microsoft Windows Vista or XP. Click **Start** and **Connect To** and follow the instructions on the screen; you may need to enter a user name and password provided by your ISP. In Windows 7 click **Start**, **Control Panel**, **Network and Internet** and **Connect to a network**.

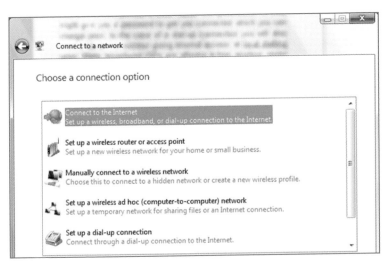

During the initial setting up process it may be necessary to have a computer connected directly to the router with an Ethernet cable. Once the router is up and running the Ethernet cable can be removed.

After installing the software from
the CD or using the **Connect To**
feature in Windows, a small
Internet icon (consisting of either
one or two monitors as shown on
the right) should appear in the

Notification Area on the Taskbar at the bottom right of the screen
in Windows XP and Vista. The icon will probably display a red
cross, indicating that the Internet is not yet connected; hover the
cursor over this icon and it should display the message **Wireless
networks are available**, as shown above. The Windows 7 icon
is shown on the right, with an orange
star, indicating that connection to the
Internet has not been made yet.

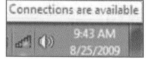

Double-click the Internet icon and from
the small window which pops up, click **Connect to a network**. A
list of nearby wireless networks is displayed, including yours, as
shown below:

In this example, two networks have been detected, **BTHomeHub
-5778** and **whitebox**, belonging to a neighbour. The name of a
network is also called the *SSID* or *Service Set Identifier* in
Internet jargon. Click the name of your connection, such as the
BTHomeHub and then click the **Connect** button, before entering
the **wireless key** given to you by your Internet Service Provider.

Entering the Security Key

The security key or password must be entered into every computer the first time it is connected to the router. If you don't have a secure network, i.e. requiring a security key, any of your neighbours or someone nearby with a laptop could use your Internet connection and possibly hack into your data. The dialogue box for entering the security key is shown below:

Type the network security key or passphrase for BTHomeHub2-SW8N

The person who setup the network can give you the key or passphrase.

Security key or passphrase:

•••••••••••

☐ Display characters

Finally Connected to the Internet

All being well, once you click **Connect** you will be told that you are successfully connected to the router and the Internet. This is also indicated by the Internet icon which should appear as shown below, depending on your version of Windows. These are found on the right of the Taskbar along the bottom of the screen.

Connected to the Internet

Windows XP   **Windows Vista**   **Windows 7**

Not Connected to the Internet

Windows XP   **Windows Vista**   **Windows 7**

Checking Your Internet Connection

Right-click the Internet icon at the bottom right of the screen, as shown on page 35 then click **Network and Sharing Center**. This dialogue box allows you to view many aspects of your new wireless network. You can also set up your network so that files, printers and other resources can be shared by all of the computers on the network.

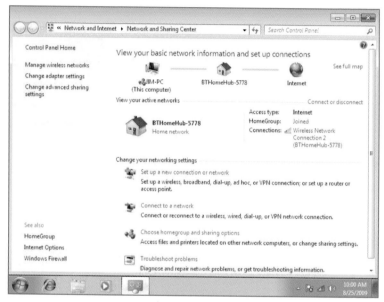

Broadband Speed

Finally you can check the speed of your broadband Internet connection. As stated at the bottom of page 29, download speeds are measured in *Megabits* or millions of *bits* per second, with performance varying from 2 to 50Mbps depending on the system. 8-10Mbps is currently considered a good broadband speed. The download speeds stated above are *nominal*; in practice these may not be achieved because of factors such as the distance of your home from the local telephone exchange.

Checking Broadband Speed

The broadband speeds quoted in ISPs advertisements are usually download speeds; this is because downloading is what the ordinary user does most of the time when using the Internet. Downloading involves opening Web pages and copying files, documents, software, music and video from the **Web server** to their **client** computer. Unless we are professional Web page designers or Web "masters", most of us spend less time uploading files to the Internet, updating Web pages or uploading new Web sites.

You can check your broadband speed by logging onto a Web site such as:

www.broadbandspeedchecker.co.uk

Now follow the instructions on the screen to test the upload and download speeds of your broadband connection.

The image below shows the result of running the speed checker on my Windows Vista computer:

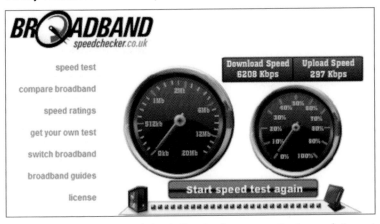

From the above speed test it can be seen that my Internet connection via a BT Home Hub wireless router has a download speed of 6208Kbps or just over 6Mbps. Note that the upload speed of 297Kbps is only a small fraction of the download speed.

The Future

Competition between Internet Service Providers and the demands of customers for more powerful systems is leading to ever faster download speeds. These greater speeds are required for the downloading of large files such as films and TV programs on demand. Not long ago most people were using a dial-up modem, forerunner to the broadband system, with a nominal download speed of only 56Kbps (Kilobits per second) or 56,000 bits per second. Now a relatively slow broadband connection of 2Mbps is still about 35 times faster than the dial-up connection, while a not uncommon 8Mbps system would be well over 100 times faster.

Virgin Media, which supplies broadband over its fibre optic cable television network, recently announced a 50Mbps (nominal) download speed. At 50 Mbps a two-hour film would take about 3 minutes to download. Dial-up would take several hours. In the future, Internet and television may converge completely in the home, with a single Internet connection providing Web browsing together with all your films and television programs *on demand*.

Broadband speeds in several other countries are currently considerably much higher than in the United Kingdom. At the time of writing, (in 2009), the Government White Paper, entitled *Digital Britain*, has set a target to enable everyone in the United Kingdom to have access to 2Mbps broadband by 2012 and 10Mbps by 2013. This might be financed by a "broadband" tax on landlines. BT is installing 40Mbps fibre optic broadband cables in various parts of the United Kingdom, starting with Scotland.

Modems in the form of *dongles* which plug into a laptop should, in theory, be able to connect to the Internet while on the move anywhere in the UK, so you don't have to find a *WiFi access point* in a hotel or station, etc. BT Mobile Broadband uses a USB dongle modem to give a 7.2Mbps download speed; this should be available to 80% of the United Kingdom.

4

Surfing the Net

Introduction

This chapter covers the use of a Microsoft Windows computer to begin exploring the Net. Windows XP, Windows Vista and Windows 7 are supplied with their own Web **browser**, known as Internet Explorer; a browser is a program for finding information and displaying Web pages. The European Parliament ruled that other manufacturers of browsers should be able to compete with Microsoft in the Windows browser market. Microsoft responded by offering a "ballot screen" allowing users of Internet Explorer a chance to download and use a different browser.

At the time of writing Internet Explorer is by far the most commonly used browser, followed by Mozilla Firefox. This chapter is based on Internet Explorer but alternative
browsers are discussed in Chapter 5. The latest version, Internet Explorer 8, can be downloaded free of charge from:

www.microsoft.com

Some of the main functions of a Web browser are:

- Displaying Web pages on the screen.
- Searching for Web pages containing specific information.
- Moving between Web pages using *clickable links*.
- Displaying Web pages after entering the *Web address*.
- Bookmarking Web pages for future reference.
- Downloading files such as videos, music and documents.

Launching Internet Explorer

From the Start Menu

Internet Explorer sits at the top of the Start Menu which is displayed by clicking the **Start** button at the bottom left-hand corner of the screen, as shown on the right.

Click over the Internet icon or the word **Internet** to launch the Internet Explorer program. The program opens at the Internet Home Page, as shown near the top of page 42.

Using the Quick Launch Internet Explorer Icon

The Taskbar is the long horizontal strip along the bottom of the screen. On the  left of the Taskbar is the **Start** button, shown above. To the right of the **Start** button on the Taskbar you may see some more icons, as shown above. On Windows XP and Vista, this is the Quick Launch toolbar and provides very easy access to various programs and features. On Windows 7 the left-hand side of the Taskbar is slightly different, as shown on the right.

Windows XP, Vista and Windows 7 all have an Internet Explorer icon, as shown on the right, on the left-hand side of the Taskbar. This allows you to start Internet Explorer with a single click of the left mouse button.

Displaying the Quick Launch Toolbar (XP and Vista)

If you can't see the Quick Launch toolbar, right-click over a blank area of the Taskbar along the bottom of the screen. From the menu which pops up select **Toolbars** and then click **Quick Launch** to make sure it is ticked, as shown below. The Quick Launch toolbar icons should now be displayed, as shown on the previous page.

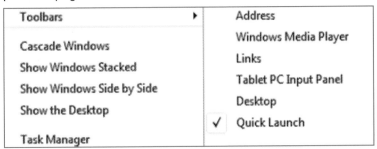

Adding Programs to the Quick Launch Menu (XP and Vista)

You can add programs to the Quick Launch toolbar by *dragging* their icons onto the toolbar. To drag a program icon, place the cursor over the icon on the Windows Desktop or on the Start Menu, then, keeping the left-hand button held down, move the cursor over the Quick Launch toolbar and release the mouse button. For example, if the Internet Explorer icon shown on the right was not present when the Quick Launch toolbar was displayed on the Taskbar.

The Home Page

Whenever you launch Internet Explorer, the computer displays the Home Page. This is often the MSN page shown on the next page, but you can use any page you like as your Home Page. This can be done using **Internet Options** from the **Tools** menu in Internet Explorer; or you can click the **Home** icon on the left of the Command Bar towards the top right of the screen, as shown below.

Changing the Home Page

When you first start up the Internet it may be displaying the default Home Page at **http://uk.msn.com/** as shown below.

However, you can change the Home Page to whatever you like. First open the Web page which is to be used as the new Home Page. Then from the Menu Bar across the top of the Internet Explorer screen, select **Tools** and **Internet Options** and make sure the **General** tab is selected. Now click **Use current** as shown below, followed by **Apply** and **OK** to set the currently open Web page as your new Home Page.

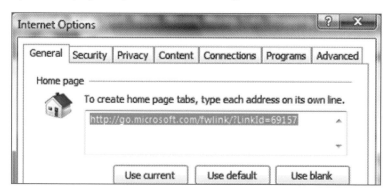

Alternatively click the arrow on the Home icon shown on the right and then click **Add or Change Home Page...** and **Use this web page as your only home page**.

Clickable Links

If you open the Home Page in Internet Explorer and move the cursor around the screen, you'll notice that the form of the cursor changes to a hand when it's over certain screen objects. Objects causing the hand to appear can be either pictures or text; the appearance of the hand indicates a *link*, also known as a *hyperlink*. While the cursor is over a text link the words are underlined as shown below for the <u>Travel</u> link. Clicking a link causes the Web browser to locate and display another Web page. This new Web page may be in another part of the current Web site or it may be on a different Web site on another Web server anywhere in the world.

The example below shows an extract from Internet Explorer 8, with links representing various categories or directories.

Sport	TV	Life & Style	<u>Travel</u>	Weather	Environment
Lottery	Jobs	Horoscopes	Games	Auctions	Shopping

Clicking the <u>Travel</u> link opens another Web page, **Travel Features**, which contains many more links, as shown in blue in the extract below.

LAST MINUTE DEALS from ebookers.com

- Worldwide city breaks from £140
- Summer holiday deals from £199
- Stay 3 pay, 2 Marriott Exclusive
- Up to 10% off worldwide car hire

- Book together and save from £199
- Mediterranean hotels from £29
- <u>Britain's hidden retreats from £79</u>
- Bank holiday deals from £135

MORE ON MSN TRAVEL

The wonders of West Sussex
Enjoy a stay-cation in Britain and enjoy views which rival the French alps.

Clicking the link **Britain's hidden retreats from £79** shown in the extract at the bottom of the previous page launches the **ebookers.com** Web site shown below.

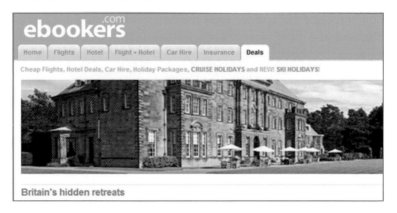

Each of the tabs shown above, such as **Home**, **Flights**, **Hotel**, **Car Hire**, etc., is a link to further Web pages allowing you to check the various services and make bookings online.

Forward and Back

When you've moved between a series of Web pages, the Forward and Back buttons at the top left of the screen display white arrows against a blue background, as shown on the right and below. These provide a quick and easy way of moving in either direction between Web pages that you've previously visited.

Starting from your own Home Page, you can move about the Internet from Web page to Web page and between Web sites all over the world. All this is achieved simply by clicking the links between Web pages.

Returning to Your Home Page

No matter how many Web pages you've visited you can always return straight back to your Home Page by clicking the Home icon on the Command Bar towards the top right of the Internet Explorer screen.

Displaying Toolbars

If the Command Bar above is not displayed on your computer, click **View** and **Toolbars** and click to make sure there is a tick against **Command Bar** (and any other toolbars you may need.)

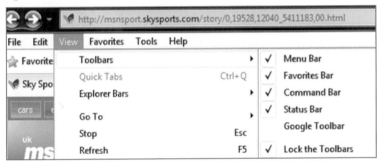

Displaying the Latest Version of a Web Page

Some Web pages have to be updated at regular intervals throughout the day. For example, when checking live flight arrivals at one of the airports your computer may not be displaying the latest updated information if the page has been loaded on your computer for quite some time. To display the latest version of a Web page, select **View** from the Menu Bar shown above and then click **Refresh**.

Surfing the Internet using the clickable links is fine for some purposes but you often need other methods to move directly to specific Web sites or find out about particular topics. These other methods are discussed in the next few pages and in Chapter 5.

Typing in a Web Address

To use this method of navigating to a Web site, you obviously need to obtain the address, perhaps from an advertisement, or newspaper article. Exact spelling and punctuation are important. Every Web site has a unique address, such as:

http://www.mycompany.co.uk/

This is entered manually into the Address Bar across the top of the Internet Explorer Web browser, as shown below:

In computing jargon, the address of a Web site is known as a **URL** or **Uniform Resource Locator**. In the above example, the meanings of the parts of the address are as follows:

http:

HyperText Transfer Protocol. This is a set of rules used by Web servers. **ftp** is another protocol used for transferring files across the Internet.

www

This means the site is part of the World Wide Web.

mycompany.co.uk

This part of the Web address is known as the *domain name*.

mycompany

This is the name of the company or organization hosting the site.

co.uk

This denotes a Web site owned by a UK company. **co** is known as the *domain type*.

Other common Web site domain types include:

biz	Business
com	Company or Commercial organisation
eu	European Community
info	Information site or service
me.uk	UK individual
org	Non-profit making organization
gov	Government
net	Internet company

In addition, some Web addresses include the code for a country, such as **fr** and **uk** as in:

www.bbc.co.uk/

If you know the address of a Web site, enter this into the Address Bar at the top of the Web browser as shown below. (In practice you can usually miss out the **http://www.** part of the address. This will be filled in automatically.)

When you press **Enter** your browser should connect to the Web site and display its Home Page on the screen. Then you can start moving about the site using the links within the page as described earlier. If you click the small downward pointing arrowhead to the left of three icons shown on the right, a drop-down menu appears with a list of the addresses of your recently visited Web sites, as shown on the next page. If you click one of the addresses it will be placed in the Address Bar and you can then connect to the Web site by pressing **Enter** (if this doesn't happen automatically).

Sometimes you may notice the icons on the right of the Address Bar will change to the group shown on the right. These have the following functions:

	Display a clickable list of previously visited Web addresses
	Use Compatibility View for older Web site designs
	Refresh the Web page with the latest information
	Stop trying to connect to the specified Web site

If you start typing a Web address that you've entered before, the browser displays a list of suggested complete addresses under the Address Bar. If the address that you require is displayed, click its entry in the list to connect to the Web site.

Searching Using the Address Bar

The next chapter covers searching the Web for information on a specific subject; this is normally done by entering the relevant *keywords* into a special program known as a *search engine*. Google is probably the most well-known search engine at the present time. However, you can enter keywords, such as **wild orchid**, for example, into the Address Bar in Internet Explorer as shown below; the default search engine then produces a list of links to Web sites containing your keywords on their pages.

Web Sites of Special Interest

There are many Web sites containing useful information for older people. The following Web addresses can be typed straight in after clicking in the Address Bar. There's no need to enter **http://** every time. Most of the Web sites give advice and information on topics such as health, finance and travel for the over 50s.

www.ageconcern.org.uk Age Concern Web Site.

www.agepartnership.co.uk Equity release specialists.

www.aarp.org Discounts, magazine and online information.

www.cennet.co.uk Holidays for the over 50s.

www.direct.gov.uk Guide to government services.

www.dwp.gov.uk Advice on benefits, work and pensions.

www.fiftyplus.co.uk Fashion catalogue for people over 50.

www.friendsreunited.com Catch up with old school friends.

www.digitalunite.com Digital Unite (DU) – computer training for the over 50s.

www.helptheaged.org.uk Support for older people.

www.kelkoo.co.uk Price checks on Internet goods for sale.

www.laterlife.com Promotes a fuller life for the over 50s.

www.moneysupermarket.com Comparisons of prices of goods and services.

www.neighbourhoodwatch.net Promotes home security.

www.nhsdirect.nhs.uk Advice and help with illness.

www.opin.org.uk Older People's Information Network.

www.overfiftiesfriends.co.uk Senior social networking.

www.primeiniative.org.uk Encourages over 50s enterprise.

www.rias.co.uk Insurance for over 50s.

www.saga.co.uk Wide range of services for older people.

www.seniority.co.uk Internet community for over 50s.

www.seniorsnetwork.co.uk News and information.

www.ship-ltd.org Release capital tied up in your home.

www.silversurfers.net Provides links to an enormous range of Web sites relevant to over 50s in particular.

www.sixtyplusurfers.co.uk Online magazine for over 60s.

www.theoldie.co.uk A witty magazine for *all* ages.

www.thewillsite.co.uk Help in making your own will.

www.thisismoney.co.uk Guide to savings and loans.

www.travel55.co.uk Holidays for older people.

www.uswitch.com Look for cheapest gas, electricity and telephone, etc.

The Keyword Search

So far we have looked at two ways of moving to different Web pages:

1. By clicking text or picture *links* on the current Web page.
2. By typing the *address* or *URL* of a Web page into the Address Bar in Internet Explorer.

The World Wide Web also enables you to find information easily on specific topics. No other source of information, such as books, magazines, etc., can match the Web for the sheer quality and quantity of information and its ease of retrieval. This is made possible by the ability to search through billions of Web pages and list those which contain certain **keywords**.

Suppose you are a bird watcher and want to find out about the **Red Kite**. Simply enter the name of the bird into the Search Bar in Internet Explorer, as shown below.

When you press **Enter** or click the magnifying glass icon above, the search program, known as a **search engine**, instantly produces a list of search results, as shown on the next page. In this example, Microsoft's Bing search engine is being used but there are many others including the world famous Google, discussed in the next chapter. Most searches only take a fraction of a second and can produce millions of results.

Each of the results in the list includes the title of the Web page, underlined and in blue; this is a clickable link to the Web page.

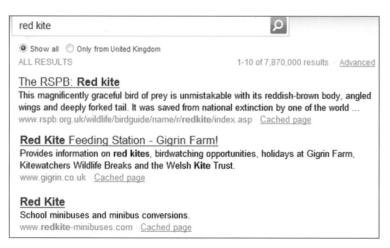

Shown above is just a very small sample of the millions of search results. In this example, the first result connects to the RSPB Web site, allowing you to see videos, hear sound recordings and read facts about the **Red Kite**.

Narrowing Down a Search

Although nearly 8 million Web pages were found containing the words **Red Kite**, not all of them are relevant to the current bird search; for example one result above is a link to a **Red Kite** bus company. Adding the word **bird** to the keywords in this case would *narrow down* the search and eliminate many such irrelevant results. Fortunately search engines usually put the most relevant results at the top of the list and you normally find the information you need very quickly.

Cached Web Pages

The Cached page links above display earlier (but probably still informative) versions of Web pages currently unavailable.

Sponsored sites

These are links to companies paying to have their names at the top of relevant search results. For example, results of searches for books will be headed by links to well-known book retailers.

More Surfing and Searching

Revisiting Web Pages

You often need to return to a Web site at a later date, such as an online bank account or supermarket shopping site. As discussed shortly, Internet Explorer automatically creates a list of links to recently visited Web pages in its *History* feature. Or you can add the current Web site to your list of *Favorites* (American spelling). (Some browsers refer to such Web site links which have been created by the user as *Bookmarks*).

Creating a Desktop Shortcut Icon

For a really quick and direct way to return to a Web page you frequently use, you can place an icon for it on the Windows Desktop. First open the required Web page and right-click over a blank area. From the menu which pops up select **Create Shortcut**. When asked if you want to place a shortcut icon to the Web site on your desktop, click the **Yes** button. In future, double-clicking the new desktop icon immediately launches the Web site, in this example online shopping at **www.tesco.com**.

Displaying the Windows Desktop

To display the Windows Desktop at any time, click the **Show desktop** icon shown on the right. This is found on the Quick Launch toolbar on the Taskbar, shown on the right, at the bottom left of the Windows XP and Vista screen. On Windows 7 the Desktop can be displayed at any time by clicking the rectangular **Show desktop** button just visible on the

extreme right of the Windows 7 Taskbar as shown on the right.

The Favorites Feature

The Favorites Bar across the top of the screen is shown below under the Menu Bar (**File**, **Edit**, **View**, etc.). The Favorites Bar lets you return to Web pages visited days or weeks before.

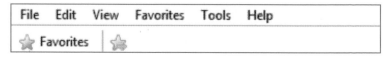

Clicking the **Favorites** button above opens a list of links to Web pages as shown on the right. These have been "bookmarked" by the user for future use. To add a Web page to the Favorites list, open the page on the screen and click **Favorites** from the Menu Bar above, then select **Add to Favorites…**. To return to this Web page at any time, simply 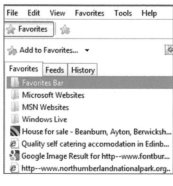 click the Web site's entry in the Favorites list. You can also add a link to the current Web site to the Favorites Bar across the top of the screen. Open the Web page, such as **Babani Books** for example, then click the star icon to the right of the word **Favorites**.

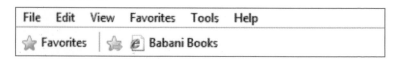

Clicking the small arrowhead next to **Add to Favorites…** shown here on the  right displays a menu enabling you to organize your Favorites into folders for different categories; you can also delete or rename them and import or export them to different computers.

The History Feature

The History feature is another list of previously-visited Web sites, but, unlike Favorites, it is created automatically by Internet Explorer. To display the History list, click

the **Favorites** button shown on the right above, then select the **History** tab as shown on the right. To return to a Web site which you've previously visited, click the entry for the site in the drop-down History list, as shown on the right. A Web site can be deleted from the History list by right-clicking the site's entry and then clicking **Delete** from the small menu which appears.

You can specify how long you wish to keep pages in the History list. From the Internet Explorer Menu Bar, select **Tools**, **Internet Options** and make sure the **General** tab is selected. Under **Browsing history** click the **Settings** button. You can now set the number of **Days to keep pages in history:**, as shown below.

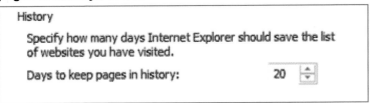

Use the small arrows shown above to increase or decrease the number of days, before clicking the **OK** button to finish. There is also a button, shown on the right, to delete all of your browsing history. This is accessed from **Tools**, **Internet Options**, the **General** tab and **Browsing history**.

Tabbed Browsing

This feature, included in Internet Explorer 7 and 8, enables you to open several Web sites in one Window. Previous versions of Internet Explorer required you to open a separate window for each Web site. Clicking the tabs makes it very easy to switch between Web sites, especially useful when you need to keep referring back to different pages.

In the example below, two tabs are open in a single Explorer window. On the left is the list of the results of a *keyword search* for the **greater spotted woodpecker**; next to it is a tab for the **Homepage for Babani Books**.

Clicking any of the tabs displays that Web page. The icon here on the right and on the left above is the **Quick Tabs** button; selecting this displays "thumbnails" or miniature images of the currently tabbed Web pages, as shown below for six tabbed Web pages. The thumbnail images help you to identify the Web page you want and then move directly to it by clicking the image. **Close** an image by clicking the cross at the top right.

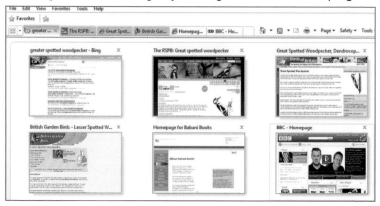

Opening New Tabbed Web Pages

When you start Internet Explorer, the name of your Home
Page is displayed on a tab. To the right of this tab is a
small blank tab; hover your cursor over the blank tab and
the **New Tab** icon appears, as shown on the right and below.

When you click the **New Tab** icon or press the **Ctrl+T** keys,
the **New Tab** itself appears as shown below, together with
the **Quick Tabs** button shown here on the right and on the
left below. (Internet Explorer 7 uses the words **Blank Page**
instead of **New Tab**, but the idea is the same.)

After opening a **New Tab**, if you type a Web address into the
Address Bar in Internet Explorer and press **Enter**, the Web page
opens and its title replaces the words **New Tab** on the tab shown
above. Several other ways to open a Web page on a **New Tab**
are listed below:

- Press the **Ctrl** key while clicking a link on a Web page.

- After typing an address into the Address Bar, (discussed
  on page 46), hold down the **Alt** key and press the **Enter**
  key, also known as the **Return** key.

- Click over a link using the *middle* mouse button (if you
  have one).

- Right-click over a link and select **Open in New Tab** from
  the drop-down menu.

The Internet Explorer Command Bar

The Command Bar is a group of icons towards the top right of the Internet Explorer screen, as shown below.

The functions of some of the icons and tools are as follows:

 The Home icon; click this to return to your Home Page at any time. Clicking the small arrowhead to the right of the icon displays the menu shown on the left, allowing you to change your Home Page or add or remove pages. See also pages 41 and 42.

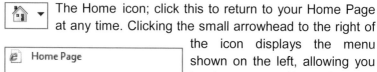

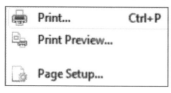 This is the **RSS Feeds** icon. Feeds are like newsflashes of the latest Web page content, such as weather information. RSS stands for Really Simple Syndication. If a Web page supplies feeds, the icon is coloured, as in the example here. A greyed out or colourless icon indicates that no feeds are available on the page.

The icon on the left launches your e-mail program to read your latest messages. E-mail is discussed in detail in Chapter 6.

Printing a Web Page

 Clicking the printer icon shown on the left allows you to make a copy on paper of the current Web page. The small arrowhead to the right of the printer icon above left displays options to **Preview** the printout on paper and adjust various page settings. These include the addition of headers and footers, changing the paper size and the *orientation* of the paper — *portrait* or *landscape* (long edge vertical or long edge horizontal.)

Saving a Web Page

The **Page** icon on the Command Bar presents a menu of options including **Save As...** to save a Web page with a name of your choice and in a selected folder location on your hard disc.

The Web page can be viewed again later by double-clicking its name in the folder in which it was saved. Other options on the **Page** menu include editing the text of the page in Microsoft Word and also e-mailing the page to a friend or colleague, etc.

Privacy and Security

The **Safety** button on the Command Bar provides various security and privacy features. These include an option to delete your browsing history and also to use the **SmartScreen Filter** to check on potential threats from another Web site, as shown below. Such threats include *phishing*, in which, for example, fraudsters try to trick you into loading a bogus Web page and then to reveal your bank account details.

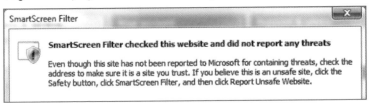

The **Safety** menu also includes a link to the **Windows Update** Web site; **Update** allows you to download the latest upgrades to the Windows operating system, including security features.

The Tools Menu

The **Tools** menu on the right of the Command Bar shown again here contains a number of important options discussed below.

The Pop-Up Blocker

Pop-ups are small windows which can suddenly appear on the screen; they often contain advertisements and can be a nuisance. Internet Explorer contains a Pop-up Blocker to allow you to prevent these interruptions to your browsing. Click **Tools** from the Command Bar shown above, and then select **Pop-up Blocker** from the drop-down menu. Now select **Turn on Pop-up Blocker** from the sub-menu shown on the right.

Turn On Pop-up Blocker

Pop-up Blocker Settings

Toolbars

The **Tools** menu on the Command Bar also has a **Toolbars** option which displays the sub-menu shown on the right. This enables you to switch the various toolbars on or off and to customize the toolbars by adding or removing buttons. For example, if you don't use the **Menu Bar** (**File**, **Edit**, **View**, etc.,), you could switch it off. (Many of the Menu Bar options are duplicated on the menus which drop-down from the Command Bar.)

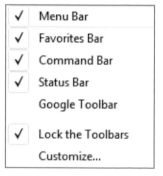

✓	Menu Bar
✓	Favorites Bar
✓	Command Bar
✓	Status Bar
	Google Toolbar
✓	Lock the Toolbars
	Customize...

The **Tools** menu also has an **Explorer Bars** sub-menu which allows you to switch the display of the **Favorites**, **History** and **Feeds** features on or off. These features appear in a panel called the Favorites Center on the left of the Internet Explorer screen, as shown on page 54.

Internet Options

This dialogue box allows you to change many of the Internet Explorer settings. You can open **Internet Options** from the **Tools** menu launched from the Command Bar shown on the previous page. The **Internet Options** dialogue box should open with the **General** tab selected, as shown below.

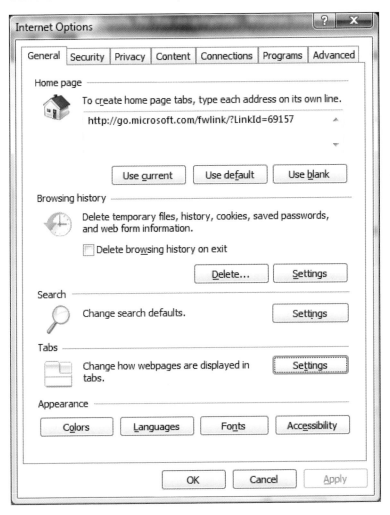

Home Page

The **General** tab shown on the previous page includes the Home Page settings as discussed earlier. You can assign a Web page as your Home Page after opening the Web page on the screen. Then open **Internet Options** and click the button marked **Use current**. Next time you start Internet Explorer the first page you see will be your new Home Page. As shown on the previous page, there is a **Use blank** button. A blank Home Page causes Internet Explorer to start up faster than a complex Home Page.

Browsing History

This section of the **Internet Options** allows you to delete from your hard disc, the names of previously-visited Web sites listed in your History feature. The **Delete...** button in the **Browsing history** section allows you to get rid of **Cookies** and **Temporary Internet Files**. These are files on your hard disc storing copies of Web pages and other information. Web pages load faster from your local hard disc than by downloading from the Internet. (When browsing, to make sure you are using the latest version of a Web page, click **Refresh** off the **View** menu on the top left of the Internet Explorer screen.) The **Settings** button under **Browse History** in **Internet Options** is used to specify how many days previously-visited Web sites stay in the History list.

Search

The **Search** section of the **Internet Options** window shown on the previous page allows you to change the default search program (or search "engine") used in the Search Bar. This bar appears at the top right of the Internet Explorer screen, as shown below. As discussed in Chapter 4, the search engine produces a list of links to Web pages which all contain the keywords entered in the Search Bar.

When you click **Settings** in the **Search** section of Internet Options shown on page 61, a list of the available search providers is displayed, as shown below:

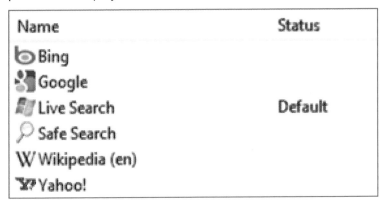

Name	Status
Bing	
Google	
Live Search	Default
Safe Search	
Wikipedia (en)	
Yahoo!	

At the time of writing, Bing is the search engine provided by Microsoft for use in Internet Explorer. At the bottom of the list shown above is a link **Find more search providers....** This presents a list of additional search providers that can be added to the above list in Internet Explorer.

Many users will be happy with the default search engine provided as standard in Internet Explorer. However, Google is currently acknowledged as the best search engine in the world, both for speed of searching and quality of results. As discussed shortly, Google has also expanded into other areas of computing.

Setting Google as the Default Search Engine

Right-click over **Google** in the above list and click **Set As Default** from the menu which appears. When you click the **Close** button, **Google** should now appear as the search engine in the Search Bar at the top right of the Internet Explorer screen, as shown below.

The Google Phenomenon

Google is famous for its world beating search engine, a highly efficient tool for finding information about virtually any conceivable subject. Google finds highly relevant Web pages to match the keyword search criteria you make up and enter into the Google Search Bar. Clickable links on these Web pages then allow you to navigate to other related Web pages.

Google was started by two students at Stanford University and has grown into a multi-national corporation on the strength of its ability to find relevant results quickly. This has enabled Google to expand into other online activities such as maps, news and e-mail. Street View in Google Maps provides panoramic views of streets, buildings, vehicles and people made by scanning the streets with cameras using fleets of vehicles all over the world. Google Earth provides satellite images from all over the globe and Google Chrome is Google's own Web browser, an alternative to Windows Internet Explorer. Google Chrome OS is a complete computer operating system designed specifically to work with the Internet and to challenge the Microsoft Windows operating system which currently prevails.

At the time of writing Google is easily the world's most popular search program and a new verb, "to Google", has entered the English language. You can start Google straightaway by entering the address **www.google.co.uk** into the Address Bar, at the top left of the Internet Explorer screen, as shown below.

When you press **Enter** the Google page is launched in Internet Explorer, as shown on the next page.

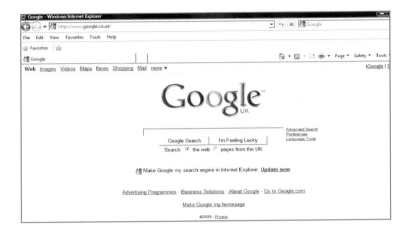

In the centre is the Search Bar into which the keywords are typed; for example, if you wanted to find information about the stormy history of the Scottish Borders, you might enter **border reivers** as your keywords, as shown below.

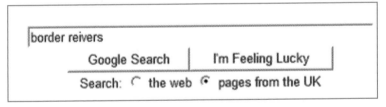

The small circular *radio buttons above* can be switched on or off with a single click to set the boundaries for the search — either the entire Worldwide Web or just pages from the UK.

Click the Google **Search** button or press **Enter** to display the list of search results, as shown on the next page.

Clicking the **I'm Feeling Lucky** button above bypasses the list of search results and opens the Web page which would have been at the top of the list of search results.

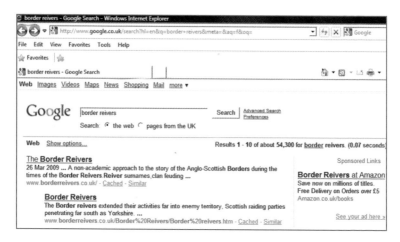

As can be seen above on the lower right, there are **Sponsored Links** to Web sites such as the Amazon online bookstore; companies pay to have sponsored links placed near the top of lists of results of searches relevant to their product or service.

Along the top of the Google search screen there is a list of various categories, as shown below. You can either search the entire **Web** or limit the search to, say, **Images**, **Maps** or **News** for example.

Launching Google Directly

Right-click over the Google screen and select **Create Shortcut** to place an icon for Google on your Windows Desktop. Whenever you want to use Google, simply double-click the icon on the Windows Desktop. If you can't see the Desktop because of Web pages or windows you've opened, click the **Show Desktop** icon as discussed on page 53.

Alternative Web Browsers

Internet Explorer is the most widely-used Web browser, being supplied with Windows XP, Vista and Windows 7. However, recent legislation in the European Parliament has meant that Microsoft now offers a choice of browsers from other manufacturers, as alternatives to Internet Explorer. This choice is implemented by a "ballot screen" provided by Microsoft, from which the user can download their chosen browser. In fact, downloading a browser without a ballot screen is a simple operation; just open the company's Web site (as listed below), click the **Download** button and follow the instructions on the screen. You might do this, for example, if you have Internet Explorer 7 on your computer and want to upgrade to Internet Explorer 8. The main browsers available for download are:

Browser	Download from Website:
Internet Explorer 8	**www.microsoft.com**
Mozilla Firefox	**www.mozilla.com**
Google Chrome	**www.google.com/chrome**
Opera	**www.opera.com**
Apple Safari	**www.apple.com**

Downloading a Web Browser (e.g. Mozilla Firefox)

Firefox is the closest challenger to Internet Explorer in the current "browser wars". You can download a free copy of the Firefox browser after entering the following into your Address Bar, as discussed on page 46 of this book.

www.mozilla.com/firefox/

Downloading a Web Browser Step-by-Step

The following method is based on Mozilla Firefox but the process is broadly the same for other browsers and software in general.

- Click the **Download** button shown on the previous page.

- From the **File Download** window click **Run** to download the **Firefox Setup** file. This may take 2 or 3 minutes.

- The downloaded setup file is placed in a temporary folder.

- In answer to **Do you want to run this software?** click **Run**.

- The setup file, initially in a compressed format for fast downloading, is extracted, i.e. expanded.

- You are presented with a **Welcome to the Mozilla Firefox Setup Wizard** which advises you to close all other applications, i.e. Programs, such as Microsoft Word.

- Click **Next** and then select **Standard** as the **Setup** type.

- Click **Next** and accept the location given for the files, then click **Install** and **Finish** to complete the process.

- An icon for **Mozilla Firefox** is automatically placed on the Windows Desktop. Double-click this icon to start Firefox at any time.

- **Firefox** is also listed on the Start Menu as shown on the right. Click the Start Button then click the **Firefox** entry on the Start Menu.

- In Windows XP and Vista an icon for **Firefox** is also placed on the right of the Quick Launch Toolbar shown on the right. A single click launches Firefox, as shown on page 69.

Mozilla Firefox at a Glance

The Firefox **Start Page** is shown above and at the centre is the Google search engine. Most of the main browsing tools appear in the top left-hand corner of the screen, as shown below.

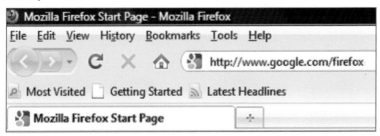

As shown above, there is the familiar **File**, **Edit** and **View** Menu Bar also including the **History** feature and **Bookmarks**. The **Tools** menu is used to alter many of the settings in Firefox. On the screenshot above, reading from the left, there are forward and back buttons and icons to reload the current page, stop loading a page and the Home button, next to the Address Bar. At the right-hand end of the Address Bar is a star icon, for bookmarking the current Web page, like adding to Favorites in Internet Explorer. The yellow button above and on the right presents the latest news. Firefox ⟨Latest Headlines⟩ includes many other features such as tabbed browsing and a pop-up blocker, as mentioned earlier in the discussion of Internet Explorer.

Choosing a Web Browser

This chapter has looked at the two most frequently-used Web browsers, Internet Explorer and Mozilla Firefox. Microsoft now provides a "ballot screen" offering a choice of browsers as alternatives to Internet Explorer. However, as discussed on the two previous pages, it's a simple matter to download any of the browsers yourself. The main alternative browsers are Mozilla Firefox, Google Chrome, Opera and Apple Safari. Any of these alternative browsers will probably be more than adequate for most users' needs, as indeed will Internet Explorer 8.

It's quite feasible to download and install several browsers and use whichever one you like. This process will normally place an icon for the browser on your Windows Desktop; if not, right-click over the entry for the browser in the Windows Start Menu and click **Send To** and then click **Desktop (create shortcut)**.

Double-click any of the Desktop icons to start surfing the Net to evaluate each browser. Some of the criteria to consider are:

- Ease of use and clarity of screens, menus, icons, etc.
- The speed with which highly relevant results can be found and displayed, using the associated search engine.
- Easy to follow and useful on-screen help.
- Useful and innovative features such as tabbed browsing, pop-up blocker and spelling checker, etc.

6

Electronic Mail

Introduction

Electronic mail or e-mail is now one of the most popular methods of communicating between people; a message consisting of text and, if necessary, pictures is entered into a computer and sent immediately to other computers anywhere in the world. Some of the main advantages of e-mail compared with the traditional letter post are:

- An e-mail travels to its destination almost instantly. If the intended recipient is online to the Internet they can read your message immediately.

- The same e-mail can be sent quickly to many different people by simply clicking their names in an electronic address book.

- An e-mail can be sent at any time – day or night.

- You don't have to make direct contact with the other person – if they're away from their computer they will see your message next time they read their mail.

- E-mails can be *forwarded* to other friends or colleagues who may be interested.

- You can send *attachments* with e-mails. These can be photographs, sound or video clips or document files containing text and pictures, for example.

- With a suitably equipped computer you can read important mail and send replies while you are away from home, anywhere in the world.

- E-mails can be saved and printed out on paper.

- Many e-mail services are free of charge.

However, there are some negative aspects to e-mail, which can cause some people a great deal of stress:

- Some people are inundated with e-mails, many of them trivial and unnecessary, yet still requiring answers.

- "Spam" or unsolicited junk mail may annoy you and clog your Inbox.

- "Phishing" e-mails attempt to trick the recipient into revealing their financial or personal details.

- An e-mail may spread a virus which can damage the files on your hard disc.

- Some e-mails tend to be written in a hurry, perhaps with less emphasis on style, content and grammar; eventually this may cause a decline in traditional letter writing skills.

- In a face-to-face meeting with someone in the same room, you can learn a lot from their demeanour, body language, tone of voice and facial expressions and possibly have a better understanding of their feelings and point of view.

In spite of these negative aspects, e-mail seems certain to remain a major method of communication, especially where speed is a factor. Important messages, perhaps concerning medical information, legal matters or business negotiations can be sent and received in minutes rather than days. For example, a doctor can e-mail some images of a medical problem to a leading specialist in another part of the world; a second opinion can be e-mailed back in a matter of minutes, possibly improving the quality of the diagnosis and speeding up the treatment.

Conversely there has been outrage when people have been dismissed from their jobs by a brief e-mail when clearly a more sympathetic and personal method of communication is called for.

E-mail Software

Microsoft Windows in the past included its own *e-mail client* software; this is a program used to type in your message then send it to its destination over the Internet. The e-mail program is also responsible for handling the messages you receive by downloading them from the Internet. Windows XP and earlier versions of Windows used the Outlook and Outlook Express programs for e-mail, while Windows Vista and Windows 7 can use Windows Mail. Windows 7 users need to download the latest version, Windows Live Mail, from the Microsoft Web site at:

http://download.live.com/wlmail

There are also third-party e-mail programs such as Eudora, Pegasus Mail and Mozilla Thunderbird.

Types of E-mail

There are two main types of e-mail, known as *POP3*, *(Post Office Protocol)* and *Web-based* e-mail.

POP3 E-mail

Your incoming messages are stored on a *mail server* computer until you read them. Then they are downloaded to your hard disc using a program such as Windows Mail or Outlook Express. Once downloaded your messages are deleted from the mail server. Advantages of this type of e-mail are that you can compose new messages and read old ones without being connected to the Internet. A disadvantage is that setting up a computer to use POP3 e-mail is quite complicated, making it difficult tor read your mail when away from home.

Web-based E-mail

This type of e-mail is handled using your Web browser, not special e-mail software; you can log on to the Web and read it using any Internet computer anywhere in the world, after entering a user name and password. Well-known Web-based e-mail services are Windows Live Hotmail and Yahoo! Mail.

Introducing Windows Mail

This is an e-mail program introduced with Windows Vista and available as a free download for Windows 7; Windows Mail is known as an *e-mail client* and replaces Outlook Express provided in Windows XP and earlier versions of Windows.

As shown below, you can launch **Windows Mail** in Vista from the **Start** menu or from the **Start**, **All Programs** menu.

Your computer may already have on icon for Windows Mail on the Vista desktop, as shown on the right. If not you can create an icon by right-clicking **Windows Mail** in the **Start** or **All Programs** menu, then select **Send To** and click **Desktop (create shortcut)**. Double-click this new desktop icon every time you want to launch **Windows Mail**.

Before sending your first e-mail, you need to enter details for your new e-mail *account*, using information provided by your Internet Service Provider such as BT, etc. Some typical information for a BT e-mail account is shown below.

E-mail address:	johnsmith@btinternet.com
Username:	johnsmith
Password:	********
POP3 Incoming mail server:	mail.btinternet.com
SMTP Outgoing mail server:	mail.btinternet.com

Setting Up a Windows Mail Account (POP3)

The first time you try to use **Windows Mail**, the setup wizard starts up and the first dialogue box requires you to enter a **Display name**, such as **John Smith**, for example, as you would like it to appear in the **From** field on the messages you send. After clicking **Next** enter your e-mail address such as **johnsmith@btinternet.com**. After clicking **Next** again enter the details of your incoming and outgoing mail servers. The servers are computers belonging to your Internet Service Provider and they handle the e-mails you send and receive. You will need to select from drop-down menus the *type* of servers, such as **POP3** for incoming mail and **SMTP** for outgoing mail. Also enter the *names* of the mail servers, such as **mail.btinternet.com** for example, as shown in the example at the bottom of page 74.

Finally click **Next** and enter the **E-mail username** and **Password** which you set up with your Internet Service Provider, together with the server details mentioned above.

Setting Up a Hotmail Account (Web-based)

Simply log on to MSN at **http://uk.msn.com** click **Hotmail** and then click the **Sign Up** button, as shown below.

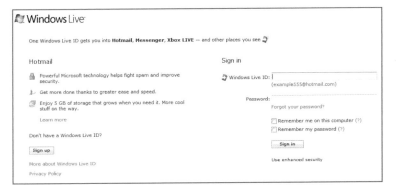

You are then presented with the **Sign up** screen shown on the next page.

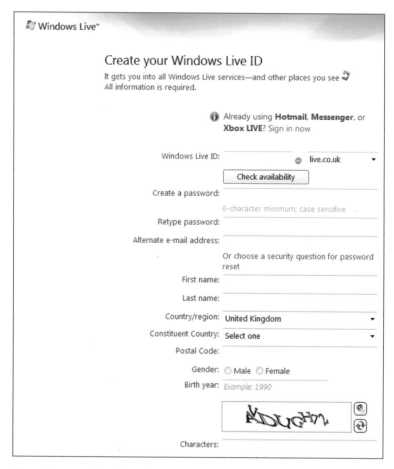

The above online form is used to set up your Hotmail user name (called the **Windows Live ID** here) and your password.

In this version of Windows Live Hotmail, an e-mail address will be something like **johnsmith@live.co.uk**. If your chosen e-mail address is not available, modify the address slightly and check its availability again. After completing your personal details and copying the jumbled verification code at the bottom, click the **I agree** button to complete the new hotmail account.

E-mail Addresses

In order to send someone an e-mail message you must know their unique e-mail address, for example:

stella@aol.com

james@msn.com

enquiries@wildlife.org.uk

richard@hotmail.com

david@live.co.uk

The first part of the e-mail address is usually part of your name, followed by the name of the mail server at your company, organisation or Internet Service Provider. The part of the e-mail address after the **@** sign is known as the *domain*. The last part of the e-mail address shows the type of organization and sometimes the country, such as:

.com	commercial company
.org	non-profit making organisations
.net	Internet company
.biz	business
.co.uk	UK business
.eu	organizations and people within EU

E-mail programs normally have an electronic Address Book or Contact List; this makes it very easy to enter the addresses of your recipients when creating an e-mail. You simply select the required e-mail addresses from the Contact List by clicking with a mouse rather than typing them at the keyboard.

The E-mail Process

The general method of sending and receiving e-mails is broadly similar whether you are using a POP3 program such as Outlook Express or a Web-based service such as Windows Live Hotmail.

The main stages in the e-mail process are as follows;

- The text of the e-mail is entered, together with a subject and the e-mail addresses of the intended recipients.

- Any *attachments* are added to the e-mail; these are files such as photos or word processing documents.

- A single click of the **Send** button despatches the e-mail to all of the recipients. You are informed if the message has been successfully delivered or otherwise.

- At this stage you can add any new recipients to your Address Book or Contact List.

- A copy of the despatched e-mail is placed in the Sent Messages folder.

- The people receiving the e-mail download and read the message plus any attachments.

- After reading the emails, the recipients can delete them, organise them into folders or print them on paper.

- A message can be *forwarded* on to other people who may be interested. You can also send a quick *reply* by typing on to the top of the original message and clicking **Send**.

Apart from the above basic tasks, an e-mail program may have additional features such as a spelling checker, an electronic calendar/planner and formatting tools for altering the style and appearance of the text and background of the message.

Using Hotmail

As this is a Web-based e-mail service, log on to the Web site at **http://uk.msn.com** and click the **Hotmail** icon. If your e-mail address doesn't appear on the screen, click **Sign in with a different account** and enter your address and password on the **Sign in** screen, which appears as shown below.

On pressing **Enter**, the **Windows Live Hotmail** Home Page opens on a tab in the Internet Explorer browser. The main folders containing e-mails are shown down the left-hand side. **Inbox** down to **Deleted** are Hotmail folders; **Jill**, **Jim**, etc., are created by the user for organising received e-mails into categories.

Creating and Sending an E-mail

From the main Hotmail screen click **New**; a blank message screen opens ready for you to start entering the names of the recipients and the text of the e-mail, as shown below.

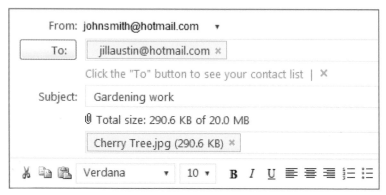

Entering the Addresses of the Recipients

First enter the names of your intended recipient(s) in the **To** bar as shown above. Each e-mail address must be spelt accurately or the message will not reach its destination. You can enter lots of e-mail addresses in the **To** bar. In Hotmail there's no need to separate the addresses with a semi-colon, etc., as you do with multiple e-mail addresses in some programs.

If some of the intended recipients are already listed in your Contact List, click the **To** button to display the list.

Then click the small box on the left of each of the required names, click **Close** and the e-mail addresses are automatically entered into the **To** bar, as shown below.

Carbon Copies: Cc: and Bcc:

In most e-mail programs there is an option to send "carbon copies" and "blind carbon copies" to people other than the main recipients. To switch these features

on click **Show Cc & Bcc** near the top right of the Hotmail screen. Two new bars for e-mail addresses, **Cc** and **Bcc**, appear under the **To** bar. All recipients can see who has received a carbon copy but the recipients of the blind carbon copies are not known to the others. After entering the e-mail addresses of the recipients, enter a meaningful word or two in the **Subject** bar.

Entering the Text

It's now just a case of entering the text of the message by typing into the main panel. There is a full range of formatting tools — bold, italic, underline, etc., bullets, numbering and coloured text and backgrounds. You can also edit text by cutting and pasting.

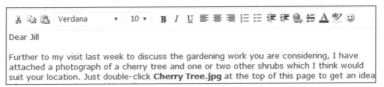

Inserting a Link to a Web Page into an E-mail

If you want a friend or relative to view a Web page, you can insert a link to the page amongst the text of the e-mail you are sending them. When your contact reads the e-mail, they simply click the link to connect their computer to the Web page. To insert a link, click the hyperlink icon shown above on the right. Enter the address of the Web page after **http://** shown on the right and click **OK** to insert the link into the text of the e-mail.

Inserting an E-mail Attachment

An attachment is a file sent with an e-mail; it might be a photograph, a financial spreadsheet or a word processing document, for example. I have sent whole chapters of books as attachments to an e-mail. It's just like using a paperclip to send a photo with a traditional letter.

When you read an e-mail, any attached files are listed at the top of the message; double-clicking the name of the file opens the file in its associated program, such as a photo editor, spreadsheet program or word processor.

To send a file such as photograph with an e-mail, click **Attach** on the Menu Bar at the top of the Hotmail screen, as shown below:

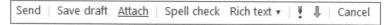

The following window opens allowing you to browse the files on your computer's hard disc to find the file to attach to the e-mail. In this case the photo **Cherry Tree.jpg** is being sent from a folder called **Garden** stored on the hard disc **(C:)**.

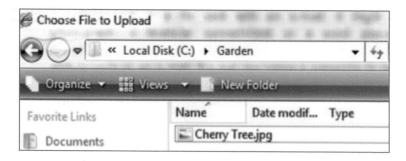

Click the required file name to select it then click the **Open** button at the bottom right of the **Choose File to Upload** window. You are then returned to the **New** e-mail screen where the name of the file, **Cherry Tree.jpg**, is displayed at the top of the e-mail message as shown in the extract on the next page.

The attached photographic file **Cherry Tree.jpg** is shown outlined in red in the image above. Several separate files can be attached and sent with an e-mail.

Sending an E-mail

When the text has been entered and any files attached, click the **Send** button to despatch the e-mail to its destination(s). All being well, the screen will display the statement **Your message has been sent**. However, if you've entered an e-mail address incorrectly or the address doesn't exist you will get a note in your Inbox from the Hotmail "postmaster" informing you that the delivery has failed.

If any of the recipients are not in your contact list you are given the chance to add them, using the small dialogue box shown on the right. Next time you send them an e-mail, you won't need to type in their e-mail address. To add them to the **To** bar just click the **To** button and click their name in the Contacts List then click **Close**.

Receiving and Reading E-mails

All incoming mail is listed in your **Inbox** as shown below. The list is displayed by clicking **Inbox** in the left-hand panel. The number in brackets indicates the number of unread messages.

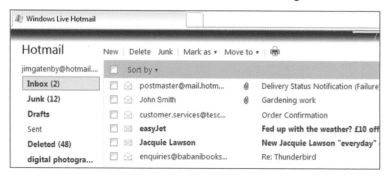

Messages which have attachments include an icon for a paper-clip after their name, as in the example below.

To read an e-mail, simply click its entry in the **Inbox** list as shown above. The e-mail opens for reading as shown below.

Opening E-mail Attachments

In the case of the **Cherry Tree** photo attached to the e-mail in the previous example, the photograph is displayed after the text of the message as soon as you open the e-mail for reading. However, you may want to open an attachment for editing. For example, if you are collaborating with someone on a report or a financial spreadsheet. Then you need to open the file in its *associated* program; for example, a word processing document in Microsoft Word, a spreadsheet file in Excel.

The screenshot on the right shows an Excel spreadsheet file **Income Expenditure 2009.xlsx** as an e-mail attachment. Click the file name and the following dialogue box appears.

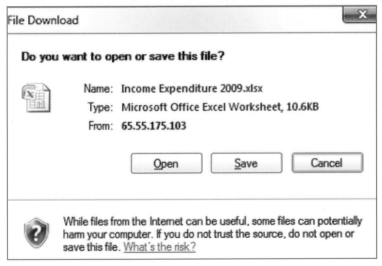

You are warned of the risks of opening or saving files from an unknown source; always make sure your computer is protected with up-to-date anti-virus and Internet security software as discussed in Chapter 8 of this book.

If you click **Open** in the **File Download** window on the previous page, the Excel program (in this example) opens to display the worksheet which was sent as an attachment. Then it can be edited and perhaps sent to someone else as an attachment. Similarly, the photo file **Cherry Tree.jpg** would be opened in a program like Photoshop Elements or whatever is your default program for **.jpg** photographic files.

Managing E-mails

There are several ways of dealing with e-mails which you've received into your Inbox. The Menu Bar across the top of the Hotmail Inbox has the following options, as shown below.

New | Delete   Junk | Mark as ▾   Move to ▾ | 🖶

Delete

Any messages you don't want to keep can be ticked in the Inbox list then deleted. The **Junk** folder contains messages deemed as junk mail and these are automatically deleted regularly.

Mark as

This option allows you to mark messages as **Read**, **Unread** or as a **Phishing Scam** if someone has been asking for personal information.

Reply, Reply All and Forward

These options allow you to deal quickly with an incoming message. Clicking **Reply** addresses the message automatically and you type in your reply above the original message. **Reply All** sends your reply to all the recipients of the message. **Forward** allows the original message to be sent on to someone else.

Move to

You can create a system of folders using **Manage Folders** near the bottom left of the Hotmail screen. **Move to** allows you to place e-mails in these folders.

7

Your Own Web Presence

Introduction

A few years ago, creating a Web site was a specialised task; each page had to be built up by writing lists of instructions in the Web page language **HTML** or **HyperText Markup Language**. As with so many computing tasks, software has been developed to shield the user from the more technical aspects; nowadays programs like WebPlus allow you to create stylish Web pages easily with all the features you'd find in a professional site. Some programs offer a *template* approach in which you choose a design from a set of ready-made Web pages. Then you simply customise the Web page by replacing the "dummy" text and pictures in the template with your own.

This chapter looks at two methods of getting your personal news and information onto the World Wide Web.

The "Blog" or Online Diary

A blog or "Web log" is a journal into which you enter text and pictures. The blog is a very simple Web site and is easy to create — the formatting, layout and uploading are done for you.

Serif WebPlus

This is a reasonably priced and easy-to-use Web design program, capable of producing professional looking results. WebPlus can be used to produce an attractive Web site to display your own news or to create an **e-commerce** site to promote a small business and deal with orders. The latest version of WebPlus typically costs about £60 and has many of the features of software costing several hundred pounds. In addition, when a new version of WebPlus is launched, Serif usually make earlier versions available as free or extremely cheap downloads from the Internet. At the time of writing Web Plus SE can be downloaded free and WebPlus10 costs £9.99.

The Blog or Online Diary

One of the best known programs is Blogger, created in 1999 and now owned by Google. If you log on to **www.blogger.com** you are given very simple on-screen instructions for creating your own blog. First you are asked to create a Google account by entering your e-mail address and password and agreeing to the Terms of Service. Then enter a title for the blog, as shown below.

Since a blog is a very simple Web site you are asked to enter the Web Address or URL (Uniform Resource Locator). The address of your blog will be something like **yourname.blogspot.com** if this has not already been used.

Blog address (URL)	http:// jimgatenby	.blogspot.com
	Check Availability	

This is the unique Web address of your blog. Your friends and relatives can connect to your blog by entering the URL in the Address Bar of their browser.

During the setup process you are given a choice of twelve Web page designs or templates on which to base your blog.

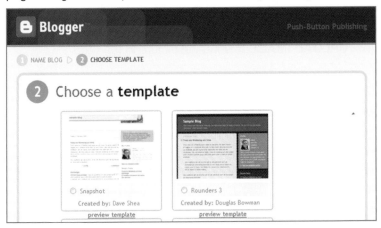

Then you're ready to start *posting* or entering the text of the blog, using the **Posting** tab in the Blogger window shown below. This has many of the features of a word-processor, including text in different styles and sizes, bold, italic, bullets, numbering and a spelling checker.

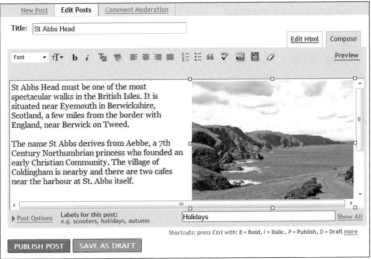

Adding a Picture to a Blog

You can insert a picture into a blog, after clicking the **Add Image** icon on the Toolbar as shown on the right and below. Browse to find the image on your computer then click **UPLOAD IMAGE** to send the picture to the Web

Previewing a Blog

Click the **SAVE NOW** button shown below to save a draft of your blog. When you've finished entering the text and pictures, click **Preview** to see what it will look like on the Web, as shown below.

Posting a Blog

Finally click the **PUBLISH POST** button shown below to post your blog on the Web for others to see. Other people can add comments to the blog and you can view the blogs of lots of other people. Blogs are free and can be used for any legitimate purpose, although a blog can be closed down if it is deemed offensive.

Creating a Web Site with Serif WebPlus

Serif WebPlus is an easy-to-use but powerful program for designing Web pages. At the time of writing you can download a free copy of the basic version, WebPlus SE, from:

www.freeserifsoftware.com

This free software has many of the features of programs costing hundreds of pounds and is capable of producing very professional Web sites. WebPlus 10 is very similar to WebPlus SE but contains additional features for creating a Web site for an online business (known as e-commerce). These features include standard forms displayed on the screen, to be completed online by customers. There are also options for managing electronic "shopping baskets" and dealing with payments. At the time of writing WebPlus 10 can be downloaded for £9.99. There are two basic approaches to creating a Web site in WebPlus:

The Template Approach

This uses a ready-made template, including pictures, text, colours and other design features. A choice of templates is available for different purposes whether business or personal. The user replaces the text and other content given in the template with their own material, while retaining the overall design and style of the template.

The Blank Canvas Approach

Using this approach you design the Web site from scratch, starting off with a blank page onto which you add your own text, images, colours and other design features. Extra pages can be inserted and all of the pages connected by the addition of *links* or *hyperlinks*, or a *Navigation Bar*.

These methods are discussed in the remainder of this chapter. On completion, the Web site must be uploaded and saved on an Internet server with a Web Address, for other people to view.

Getting Started with Serif WebPlus

When WebPlus is installed on a computer, an icon is placed on the Windows Desktop as shown on the right. Double-click this icon to launch the program. The Startup Wizard appears in the centre of the WebPlus screen, displaying the following options:

- Use a design template.

- Start from scratch.

- Open a publication.

- View tutorials.

As can be seen above there are options to use a ready-made template, start from scratch with a blank page or open an existing publication, a Web site created earlier. **View tutorials** displays some very comprehensive notes in the *Adobe PDF* format. If you have the freely-downloadable program *Adobe Reader* program you can view these notes and print them out on paper.

Using a Web Page Template

If you choose the first option **Use a design template**, you are presented with a set of ready-made templates in different styles.

If you would like to base your Web site on one of the templates, click the thumbnail image of the template as shown on the previous page and then click the **Open** button. The template opens in the WebPlus design screen, as shown below.

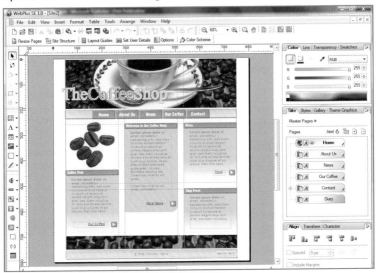

Down the left-hand side of the screen are various tools such as:

Insert text in a frame.

Insert a picture e.g. from a folder on your hard disc.

Insert a link or hyperlink to connect to another Web page.

Crop or trim a picture or image.

There are several other tools on the left-hand side including those to insert sound clips, Navigation Bars and *RSS feeds*.

Across the top of the WebPlus screen is the familiar Menu Bar with **File**, **Edit**, **View**, etc. There are options for starting a Web page on a blank sheet and opening an existing Web page that you have created and saved.

Several icons across the top of the screen are used in the development and final publishing of a Web site, as follows:

 Publish the Web site to a folder on your hard disc. This prepares the site for posting to the Internet.

 Preview your Web site, i.e. see what it will look like in any of your installed Web browsers such as Internet Explorer or Mozilla Firefox.

 Publish the finished Web site to the Web server computer you have chosen to host your Web site.

The WebPlus Studio

The Studio is a panel down the right-hand side of the screen and shows the structure of the pages that make up the Web site. All Web sites have a Home Page, which is the first page to appear when you launch a Web site. The small eye icon shows that the Home Page is currently open for editing in WebPlus. To switch to another page such as **Our Coffee**, double-click the title in the Studio.

The page title **Our Coffee** in the Studio is now preceded by the icon for an eye, as shown on the right, indicating that this page is now open for editing.

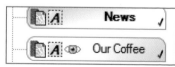

The WebPlus screen now displays the **Our Coffee** Web page ready for editing, as shown below.

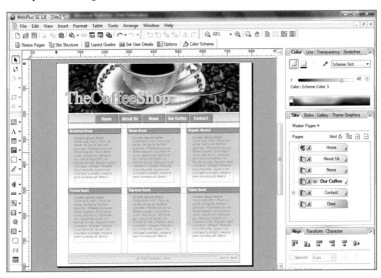

Master Pages

In this example, the artwork including the coffee cup at the top of the page appears on all six of the Web pages. There is also a Navigation Bar on every Web page, as shown below.

The Navigation Bar contains a set of links to all of the Web pages on the site. As the Navigation Bar and the coffee cup artwork appear on several Web pages, they are created on a WebPlus Master Page, which can be applied to some or all of the ordinary Web pages. Master Pages can be added and managed using the **Master Pages** area in the Studio on the right of the WebPlus screen.

Editing a WebPlus Template

Replacing the Default Text

The text in WebPlus is contained in several separate frames, as shown below. Select the required frame by clicking anywhere over the text; the selected text appears highlighted with eight blue squares, as shown on the right below.

With the text frame selected as shown above, you can now delete the default text and enter your own, just as you might edit a document in a word processor or desktop publishing program.

Replacing a Default Picture

To replace the coffee beans image shown above, select the image and then click the **Insert Picture** tool shown on the right. You are then able to browse for the new picture in its location on your hard disc, etc. Select the required image and click **Open**. Then, keeping the left-hand mouse button held down, drag the cursor (now in the shape of a cross) until the new image is the correct size, as shown below.

Starting from Scratch

Double-click the WebPlus icon on the Windows Desktop, as shown on the right, and then select **Start from scratch** from the Startup Wizard which appears. WebPlus presents you with a blank page.

Entering Text

Click the **HTML Frame Tool** shown on the right and enter your text in the frame in the required size and font.

The yellow background to the text can be applied after selecting the text frame then clicking **Format** and **Fill...** from the WebPlus Menu Bar. Select the required fill colour and click **OK**.

Inserting a Picture

Click the **Insert Picture** icon shown on the right, then browse to find the picture in a folder on your hard disc.

If the image is not likely to need updating, switch on **Embed picture** as shown on the right. This will simplify uploading and updating the Web site.

Now use the cross cursor as shown on the right to position
the image and, by keeping the left-hand mouse button
held down, drag it to the required size, as shown below.

Adding Extra Web Pages

From the WebPlus Menu Bar
select **Insert** and **Page...**; the
following dialogue box appears,
allowing you to enter a title for
the new Web page, such as
Places of Interest shown on the
right. You can also apply a
Master Page to the new page,
such as a master page
containing a Navigation Bar.

As new pages are added to the Web site, they appear in the site structure in the Studio panel as shown on the right. The new page can appear before, after or as a *child* (sub-page) of an existing page. In this example, **Edinburgh Castle** is a child of **Places of Interest**.

Inserting Links

A picture or a piece of text can be made into a link to another Web page on your site or a link to an entirely different site. For example, to make a link from the **Home Page** to the **Places of Interest** page, insert a text frame with the required words and select it. Next click the **Hyperlink** icon shown on the right to open the following dialogue box.

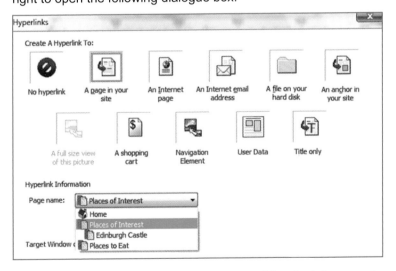

In the **Hyperlinks** window above, we would select **A page in your site** and then, perhaps, **Places of Interest**, from the drop-down menu next to **Page name:**. Click **OK** to create the link.

Creating a Navigation Bar

The Navigation Bar is a horizontal or vertical set of links between your various Web pages, created semi-automatically for you in WebPlus. First open a **Master Page** by double-clicking, e.g. **Master A**, in

the Studio then select the style, colours and design from **Theme Graphics** in the Studio. WebPlus automatically adds the names of your Web pages to the Navigation Bar, as shown below.

The Navigation Bar is part of a Master Page and this can be applied to all of the Web pages on the site or just to selected pages using the Master Page Manager in the WebPlus Studio.

Previewing a Web Site

To test any links and Navigation Bars, you need to preview the site in your installed Web browser, such as Internet Explorer or Mozilla Firefox. If you've more than one installed browser, click the small arrow next to the **HTML** **Preview** icon shown on the right and on the Toolbar above right. Then select the required browser from the drop-down list as shown on the right. This displays your Web site

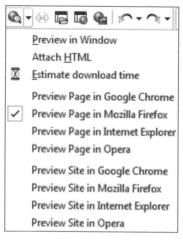

as it will appear when people open it on the Web. If necessary go back to WebPlus and edit the pages to incorporate any modifications arising from the preview.

Saving a Web Site

While you are developing a Web site, it's a good idea to regularly save a copy of the latest version of the site on your hard disc. When the site is up and running on the Web it's still advisable to keep a local copy containing the latest modifications.

To save a copy of the Web site click the **File** and **Save As...** options from the WebPlus Menu Bar. The file is saved with the extension **.wpp** as in **Edinburgh.wpp** shown below. **.wpp** is an abbreviation for **WebPlus Project**.

To save the Web site quickly keeping details such as **File name** and folder location the same as before, simply click the Toolbar disc icon shown on the right.

Publishing a Web Site

A Web site can be published to a local folder on your hard disc or to the World Wide Web. Publishing converts all the HTML text files and graphics files to the final form required by the World Wide Web. To publish a site to a local folder on your hard disc, click the **Publish to Disk** icon shown on the right, then select the destination folder and the Web pages to be published for your site.

Publishing to the World Wide Web

This requires the following to be provided by your Internet Service Provider or a specialist *Web hosting* company:

- Space on their Web server to store your Web site.
- The FTP (File Transfer Protocol) address of their server, such as **ftp://ftp.myhost.uk.net/**.
- The Web address or URL (Uniform Resource Locator) of your site, such as **www.myownwebsite.co.uk/**.
- Your personal Username and Password.

Full instructions for uploading your Web site should be available from your ISP or Web host. WebPlus has its own program for uploading Web sites, launched by clicking the **Publish to Web** icon shown on the right. After making up your own **Account** name, enter the **FTP address** of your host Web server and also your **Username** and **Password**. Finally enter your Web site **URL** and click **OK**. The following window appears, from which you click the **Upload** button to send your Web site up to the host server.

Security Matters

Introduction

The Internet has brought major changes to the lives of many people both at work and at leisure; these include instant e-mail communication, access to infinite amounts of information and the ability to shop and carry out financial transactions at the touch of a button. However, these incredible opportunities bring with them some serious risks; the sophisticated modern criminal doesn't need to break into your home armed with a jemmy. The computer felon can carry out their offences secretly from within the comfort of their own home. Listed below are some of the risks we run when using the Internet:

- A "hacker" might gain access to your computer and copy files containing personal or financial information.

- A virus, perhaps sent in an e-mail, might destroy files, wipe the hard disc and cause great inconvenience.

- If you are using an **unsecured wireless router**, unscrupulous people nearby can log on and use your Internet connection.

- You may be the target of a **phishing** attack in which criminals attempt to trick you into revealing details such as bank account numbers and passwords, etc.

Although these threats are real enough, they can be overcome by making full use of the security features within Windows XP, Vista and Windows 7, supplemented by inexpensive third party anti-virus and Internet security software as discussed shortly.

The Windows Security Center

You can check all the security features in Windows by launching the **Windows Security Center**. Click **Start**, **Control Panel** and double-click the **Security Center** icon as shown on the right. In Windows 7 click **System and Security**. You are recommended to make sure that the main security features are either switched **On** or marked **OK**, as shown below.

Security Center

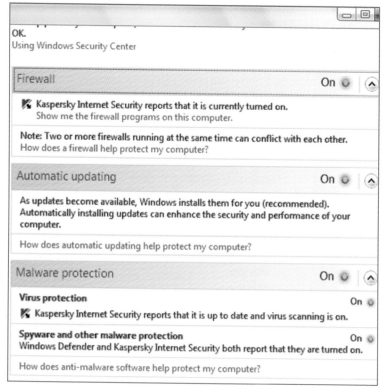

This particular computer has the popular Kaspersky Internet Security (including a *firewall*) and anti-virus software installed. Windows does not include its own anti-virus software but does include the **Windows Firewall**.

The Windows Firewall

The firewall is a piece of software or hardware designed to protect your computer from hackers and malware (malicious software). Windows has its own firewall software which should be turned on, unless you're installed an Internet security package such as Kaspersky, Norton, F-Secure or McAfee.

Turning Windows Firewall On

Select **Start**, **Control Panel**, then double-click **Windows Firewall** and click **Change settings**. If necessary click the circular radio button to make sure **Windows Firewall** is **On**. In Windows 7 select **Start**, **Control Panel**, **System and Security** then **Windows Firewall**.

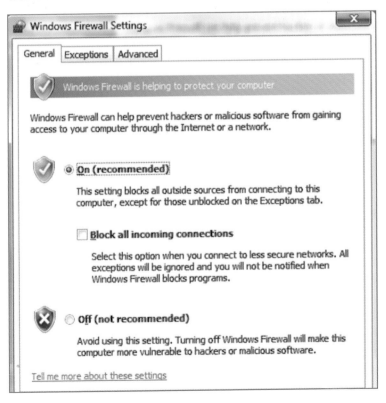

Automatic Updating

Windows Update provides regular modifications to the Windows operating system; these modifications are often designed to make the system more secure or improve performance and usually take the form of a small piece of software or "patch". **Windows Update** allows you to schedule your computer to check for the latest updates and download them to your computer from the Internet.

Windows Update can be launched from the **Start** menu; click **Control Panel** and double-click the **Windows Update** icon shown on the right. The **Windows Update** screen opens as shown below and displays the status of your updates. In Windows 7, select **Start**, **All Programs** and **Windows Update**.

You are informed when **Windows Update** last checked for available updates and the date when updates were actually installed. **Check for updates** above on the left-hand side allows you to carry out an immediate, unscheduled check for available updates. Some updates are optional while others are essential.

Change settings, shown on the left of the image above enables you to schedule automatic daily or weekly checks for updates, as shown on the next page.

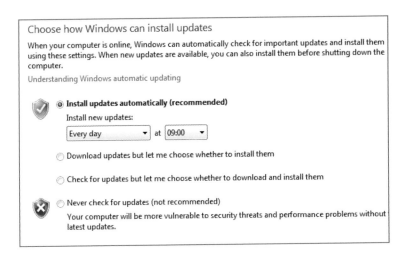

The circular "radio buttons" above allow you to choose whether you want automatic installation of updates or to control the downloading and installation yourself.

Clicking **View update history** shown on the left of the image on the previous page shows the updates that have been installed on your computer. The list can be scrolled to view almost an entire year of updates.

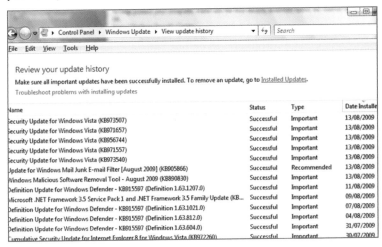

Malware Protection

Malware is an abbreviation for malicious software and refers to computer viruses and other malevolent programs; the computer virus is a small program written for the purpose of causing damage and inconvenience. In the worst case it might cause the entire contents of a hard disc to be wiped.

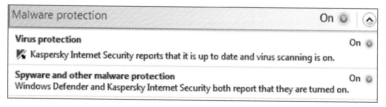

The **Malware protection** extract from the **Windows Security Center** in Windows Vista shown above reports on the status of any Internet security and anti-virus software installed on your computer. It's essential that you have an anti-virus program installed and this should have a database which is regularly updated with the latest virus definitions. Then the program can detect and destroy the latest viruses as well as many thousands of older ones.

Well known providers of anti-virus software include Kaspersky, Norton (Symantec), McAfee, F-Secure and AVG. Many companies also produce complete Internet security packages which include anti-virus software as well as firewalls and protection against *spyware* – software designed to collect personal information from a computer.

Anti-virus/Internet security packages typically cost £20 – £50 and this usually includes the software on CD or DVD and a year's updates of virus definitions. Updates are normally downloaded automatically from the Internet. Many companies now allow one software package to be legally installed on up to three computers. Subscriptions to an anti-virus package are normally renewed annually.

Kaspersky Internet Security

The Kaspersky software package gives total protection for your computer including anti-virus software as well as protection from hackers and "spyware". Spyware is illegal software installed on your computer via the Internet. This can monitor your Web surfing, detect passwords, etc., alter settings and take control of some aspects of your computer. Kaspersky Internet Security can currently be purchased for under £30 and may be installed on up to 3 computers running Windows Vista or XP.

As shown above, Kaspersky Internet Security protects files from viruses and there is a **Firewall** to keep out hackers. The Kaspersky database of known viruses is automatically updated on your computer when new viruses are discovered. Links within e-mails to known *phishing* sites are automatically blocked.

Phishing

This is a scam in which the fraudsters try to make you reveal personal financial information like your bank account and credit card numbers and passwords. The fraud often takes the form of an e-mail which may ask you to click a link to a Web site. This Web site may be a forged copy of a genuine bank or credit card company site and may look very authentic. Next you are asked to enter your personal details to "update" your records; the criminals can then use your credit card or steal money from your account.

Genuine banks and other organisations state that they never ask you to "update" or "verify" your account details by e-mail.

Web browsers like Internet Explorer and Firefox have security software to detect suspicious Web sites and check them against lists of known phishing sites. In Internet Explorer 8 select **Tools** and **SmartScreen Filter**, and make sure the **SmartScreen Filter** is turned on, using the **Turn On** option shown below.

Mozilla Firefox has phishing protection turned on by default and you can check the settings by selecting **Tools**, **Options** and **Security...** from the Firefox Menu Bar.

To prevent blocking sites which you trust and know to be genuine, their Web addresses can be added to a list of safe sites after selecting the **Exceptions...** button in Firefox, shown above.

Wireless Network Security

Wireless broadband routers have greatly improved most people's Internet experience but, without adequate precautions, your network of one or more computers may be insecure. This is because anyone, such as a near neighbour with a wireless-enabled computer or someone in the street with a wireless laptop, may be able to detect your network and use your Internet connection. As shown below, my computer has detected my **BTHomeHub** plus two networks belonging to neighbours. One of these is about 30 metres away and is listed as an **Unsecured network** in the **Connect to a network** feature in the **Windows Network and Sharing Center**, as shown below.

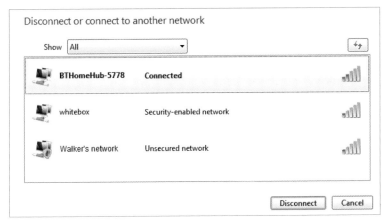

Although a firewall should stop anyone getting access to your computer and its files, it's possible for a determined hacker to intercept your network "traffic", including for example, files which you have e-mailed.

Making a home or small business network secure usually involves setting up a *wireless key*, or password. Also data files (such as financial spreadsheets) are *encrypted* i.e. scrambled to make them incomprehensible to any hackers eavesdropping within the range of your wireless network signals.

Summary: Security Matters

- Use the **Security Center** in Windows Vista, XP and Windows 7 to turn on the **Windows Firewall** to prevent hackers from getting access to your files. Alternatively install a firewall from a 3rd party company as part of a complete Internet security package. This should also include protection against *spyware* and *phishing*.

- Install anti-virus software which is regularly updated to detect and eradicate the latest viruses. (This may be part of an Internet security package mentioned above).

- Make sure that **Automatic Updates** is turned on in the **Windows Security Center**, so that you automatically receive the latest modifications intended to improve Windows security and performance.

- If using a wireless router, make sure it is on a *secure network* which uses *encryption* and requires a *wireless security key* to gain access. Otherwise people nearby can log on to your Internet connection. The Web site for the manufacturer of your router should explain how to make your network secure.

- Never disclose bank account details or passwords, etc., in response to an apparently genuine e-mail or a Web site purporting to be from a bank or credit card company, etc. Make sure your computer has protection against this activity, known as *phishing*. Genuine banks don't send e-mails asking for such information.

- Make sure passwords and "memorable" words used to access your accounts are obscure and cannot easily be guessed; passwords should be changed regularly.

- Try not to stay logged on to your bank account any longer than necessary; don't walk away and leave the computer online to the Internet.

A Glossary of Internet Terms

Access Point
A wireless connection, e.g. in an airport, enabling a computer to connect to the Internet.

ADSL
Technology used to deliver a fast broadband service over copper telephone wires, using an ADSL modem. (ADSL stands for Asymmetric Digital Subscriber Line).

Broadband
A fast Internet service using modified telephone exchanges and, in some areas, fibre optic cables.

Cookie
A small piece of text stored on your computer by your browser, recording details about your browsing habits.

Dial-up
A relatively slow Internet service, largely superseded by broadband.

Download
Transfer information and files from an Internet server to your computer; for example, e-mails, music, photographs, videos and computer software.

E-mail
Text messages sent between computers; e-mails can include *attachments* – files containing images or documents, etc. E-mail may be Web-based, such as Hotmail, or POP3, which uses special *mail servers*.

Encryption
Encoding data so that it can't be read if intercepted.

Favorites
A list of links in a Web browser which connect to Web sites which the user has "bookmarked" for future reference.

Fibre optic cabling
Special cabling used for very fast broadband services instead of the standard copper cables.

Firewall	*Software* in Windows and Internet security packages to prevent unauthorised entry to a computer; a *hardware* firewall is built into some wireless routers.
Google	The most popular search engine; also Google Earth (satellite images and Street View), Google Maps, Google Chrome (browser) and Google Chrome O.S. (operating system).
History	A list in a Web browser containing links to Web sites visited on previous days.
Home Page	The first page you see at the start of a session.
HTML	Hypertext Markup Language used to create Web pages, manually or using page design software.
Internet	Millions of computers connected globally by phone lines, satellite links and wireless.
Internet Explorer	Microsoft Web browser used for searching for information and displaying Web pages.
Internet Service Provider	Company providing Internet connections for customers via their Web servers, e.g. BT, AOL, Virgin. Some ISPs provide *content*, such as news and information.
Keywords	Relevant words typed into the Search Bar of a Search Engine when looking for information.
Link or Hyperlink	A piece of text or a picture on a Web page which can be clicked to open another Web page or Web site.
Megabit	A million *bits* (binary digits 0 and 1). A measure of broadband speed, e.g. 8 Mbps (Megabits per second).
Microfilter	Small "splitter" device allowing broadband and a telephone handset to be used simultaneously.

Modem	A device which enables binary data from a computer to be transmitted over telephone or television cables.
Netbook	Very small, inexpensive but capable laptop machine.
Online	Connected to the Internet.
PDF File	Format used for document files which can be read on any computer using free Adobe Reader software.
Phishing	A scam e-mail which tries to obtain your bank details, etc., often involving a fake bank Web site.
Plug-in	A small program, (normally a free download), used to play videos, music and animations. Examples include RealPlayer and Macromedia Flash.
Pop-ups	Small advertisements which appear unexpectedly. Some browsers contain built-in *pop-up blockers*.
RSS feeds	Newsflashes or updates to the Web page content which appear automatically on some Web sites.
Search engine	A program such as Google, Yahoo! and Bing, used to find information based on a keyword search.
Security key	A string of characters which must be entered before a computer can connect to a *secure* wireless router.
Server	A computer on the Internet to which users connect to obtain information and to download or upload files.
Spyware	Malicious software which secretly monitors users' activity.
Tabbed browsing	Opening several Web sites in a single window with tabs enabling fast switching between Web sites.
Uploading	Sending files and information, e.g. e-mail, music and photographs, from your computer to an Internet server.
USB dongle	A device which plugs into one of the rectangular ports (or sockets) on a computer.

Virus	Small malicious program (*malware*) causing damage to files and inconvenience, often sent in an e-mail.
Web address	A string of letters and dots which identifies a Web site. For example, **www.babanibooks.com**.
Web browser	A program, e.g. Internet Explorer, Mozilla Firefox, which finds and displays Web pages.
Web page	A single "sheet" on a Web site containing text, pictures and links to other Web pages and sites.
Web site	A set of Web pages on a Web server, usually representing an individual or organisation and accessed by its unique Web address or by hyperlinks.
WiFi	An international standard agreed for wireless devices, aimed at improving compatibility.
WiFi hotspot	A wireless *access point* in a hotel, etc., providing a connection to the Internet.
Windows Update	Regular downloads to your computer of latest modifications to Microsoft Windows.
Windows	The most widely used computer operating system, software which controls the computer.
Wireless network adaptor	An internal expansion card or a plug-in "dongle" enabling a computer to connect to the Internet via a wireless router or wireless access point.
Wireless router	A device which allows several "wireless-enabled" computers to share a single Internet connection.
World Wide Web	Millions of Web sites on the Internet, each site containing one or more Web pages.

Index